The Armor Of Amaterasu Ohkami

Warlock Asylum

Copyright © 2014 Messiah-el Bey

All rights reserved.

ISBN: 1495454991
ISBN-13: 978-1495454998

- INTRODUCTION 1
- THE ORIGIN OF VASUH 7
- ZHEE MUDRA 12
- AUM MUDRA 16
- TUU MUDRA 19
- THE THREE PURE ONES OF NINZUWU-SHINTO 21
- HMU MUDRA 24
- BNHU MUDRA 28
- PHE MUDRA 31
- NZU MUDRA 34
- LEWHU MUDRA 38
- SHKI MUDRA 41
- THE EMPOWERMENT OF TAKAMA NO HARA 46
- THE ARMOR OF AMATERASU OHKAMI 48
- WALKING WITH THE SUN 51
- CREATING A SHRINE OF NINZUWU 52
- THE RITE OF THE DRAGON PALACE 55
- THE DIVINE POWERS OF NYARZIR 61
- THE ART OF THE CROW (TELEPORTATION) 67
- EDITOR'S NOTES 69

ACKNOWLEDGMENTS

I would like to extend blessings and thanks to my wife, family, and all who have persevered in the Practice of the Art of Ninzuwu.

Introduction

Congratulations! It is truly a privilege and blessing to be able share in the Art of Ninzuwu today. This is a very valuable opportunity indeed. We live in a very crucial time in the history of humanity. Although we enjoy improved living conditions, due to advancements in technology affecting life overall, people still suffer from the same problems that have plagued mankind for thousands of years. Many, in hopes of finding some answers about the meaning of life, have turned to the occult.

Unfortunately, there exist many occult organizations, who only seek to capitalize on their followers' ignorance. Their methods of attracting such gullible folk are quite easy to identify actually. They will promote themselves as the being something that has already gained a legendary reputation in the eyes of the public. They do this to make their members feel like they are associated with some secret society and have joined the ranks of the powerful.

After they have convinced their flock that they are something they are not, the next step is to get them to believe in a philosophy that will isolate them from others. The reason for this is to insure that the membership cannot be "convinced otherwise" by someone who is not part of the group. Usually this "philosophy of self-isolation" comes in the form of "me-ism," or other ideologies that promote the "it's all about me" mentality. Only a person who is unaware can be convinced of such. Every pleasure that we enjoy today was created by a team of human beings working together. We no longer have to hunt for our food. We can just pick up what we need from the supermarket. However, for us to even be able to shop for food in a supermarket requires human teamwork. It takes a number of people to make a supermarket work. This is true for many things in life. The world as we know it is coming to understand this more and more. There is no pleasure in life that is produced exclusively by an individual. Shinto acknowledges the intelligence in all things. All things have a level of consciousness. This means that if a person enjoys a sunny day, or a relaxing seat next to the water, they are still in a shared experience with other conscious entities, like the sun, or a body of water. Me-ism is not a way of life for those who are spiritually aware.

People who follow these types of occult organizations betray themselves for an idea of what they are that was sold to them by the same group. It's very said indeed. In the long run, they become part of an occult organization that is doing the same thing as other occult organizations. The members of these occult organizations talk about how different they are from other groups and society in general. In differentiating themselves from others, they are doing the same thing as every other group. Sadly, the members of these occult organizations never learn about the occult, but dedicate themselves to an idea that attracted them to these very same organizations to begin with. This is just one side of the coin. On the other side of the coin, there are the happy-faced hippies of spirituality. They make it a habit of studying conclusions and repeating nice sayings they have read in books. They seem to have a positive perspective on life until you begin to notice that everything around them looks like them. They do not know how to communicate to people who live outside of their group. Instead of developing their spirituality, they develop spiritual prejudice.

It is true that when a person grows spiritually they begin to see behind the veil of world-thought and its negative emanations. This is understood by those who are sincere in the work. However, there are many who use the appearance of spirituality as a form of escapism. These types can be easily recognized because they fall into the work of the false ego. It is a religion unto its own self. Instead of focusing on working on themselves, they find a way to avoid such by seeking to impress others. This desire of impressing others is a form of mental-illness that is a result of one's addiction to the world of entertainment.

These people are ignorant to the disease that they have contracted. It is not a "showy" desire of impressing others that we are talking about here, but the justification of one's own mechanicalness. In this case, the person lives are filled with constant stories of what happened to them. Their whole life is spent telling other people about how they are the heroes of their own experience like some TV drama. "I had to tell so and so this." "I told you that already." Statements such as these and the constant projection onto others that they themselves are indeed something special, prevents them from engaging in the true work and reveals that they are just a part of "world-thought" in all their spiritual-ness, as everyone else. These new age hippies are nothing more than psychic vampires. In order for them to justify their false ego, they must gain an audience to listen to them. The listener must now use their energy and draw up an image in their minds of the speaker's story. In normal communications of this type, there is an interchange of such currents, but not for those who worship the false ego. In the end, they expect you to be just as emotionally devastated as they were during their experience.

The work of a true occultist revolves around the development of self to aid the evolution of the universe. Our universe is the result of intercourse held between two 4th dimensional universes. Our 3rd dimensional universe is growing. It is evolving into a fourth dimensional being like the parents who are responsible for its conception. Instead of thinking about impressing others," the true occultist ponders on how they can aid in this process.

Questions about the origin of our universe have often been pondered by many who live in the space of "world thought." Yet, there has also existed a body of mystics who are aware of our beginnings and purpose in the universe. In ancient times, these mystics used mythology and symbolism as a way of preserving this "sacred knowledge." We are told in the Nihongi that our universe began as "an egg" and went through several stages, similar to the human embryo. It later goes on to say the following:

"The purer and clearer part was thinly drawn out, and formed Heaven, while the heavier and grosser element settled down and became Earth."

This history, as recorded in the Nihongi, was also reported in the earlier Jomon period. In the Ivory Tablets of the Crow, we read:

"Quf agreed with what the fiery ones had spoken concerning the creation of a world that exits in time. He went down to the River of Shadows and dipped his finger in the Egu. With one drop of water he created a dimension that rested between the worlds of death and immortality."

According to both, the Nihongi and the Ivory Tablets of the Crow, the latter is a text outlining the principle spirituality of the Jomon period, our universe began as "an egg," from an infinitesimally small point and began to expand outwards. The Nihongi continues:

"Of old, Heaven and Earth were not yet separated, and the In and Yo not yet divided. They formed a chaotic mass like an egg which was obscurely defined limits and contained germs.

The purer and clearer part was thinly drawn out, and formed Heaven, while the heavier and grosser element settled down and became Earth.
The finer element easily became a united body, but the consolidation of the heavy and gross element was accomplished with difficulty."

In the passages cited above, the Nihongi describes the formation of Heaven, which was space itself but goes on to mention that Earth, or matter, took a longer period in being formed. It is interesting that in the Nihongi we not only see the creation of matter, Earth, but of space itself, the purer and clearer part. This is also expressed in the Ivory Tablets of the Crow:

"With one drop of water he created a dimension that rested between the worlds of death and immortality."

What is interesting about all of this is that modern science has confirmed the accuracy of the creation epic found in Shinto physics. In an online article, entitled, *Big Bang: How Did the Universe Begin?* by Yuki D. Takahashi, we read:

"According to the big bang theory, the universe began by expanding from an infinitesimal volume with extremely high density and temperature. The universe was initially significantly smaller than even a pore on your skin. With the big bang, the fabric of space itself began expanding like the surface of an inflating balloon – matter simply rode along the stretching space like dust on the balloon's surface. The big bang is not like an explosion of matter in otherwise empty space; rather, space itself began with the big bang and carried matter with it as it expanded."

Here we see that the modern-day Big Bang theory, is not only in full accord with earlier Shinto thought, but validates its creation epic. Modern scientists believe that the universe began as an infinitesimal point, "an egg," or as Takahashi wrote in his article "smaller than even a pore on your skin." Another feature of the Big Bang Theory and Shinto thought that puts these similarities beyond the scope of coincidence is that space, or "Heaven," was said to develop at this time as well. Takahashi states in the article:

"..space itself began with the big bang and carried matter with it as it expanded."

The Nihongi states:

"The purer and clearer part was thinly drawn out, and formed Heaven, while the heavier and grosser element settled down and became Earth. The finer element easily became a united body, but the consolidation of the heavy and gross element was accomplished with difficulty."

This shows us that the ideas expressed in the Big Bang theory were known to ancient Shinto practitioners centuries earlier. While modern science still struggles with understanding the "cause" of the Big Bang, ancient alchemists of the Jomon period recounted in their history the origin of such. The Ivory Tablets of the Crow discusses this in its symbolism, upon which we read:

"The fiery ones found much joy in the powers of arousal and spoke amongst themselves about creating a Space between the Spaces. They summoned a great scientist, who is skilled in a form of alchemy of the strange. His name is that of the Nzu-Zhee-Nzu (fire) Quf."

In Ninzuwu-Shinto mythology, the creation of this universe was planned by the "fiery ones." Hence they called upon a scientist named "Quf," in order to complete the task. This entity "Quf" has many correspondences in Ninzuwu-Shinto cosmology. We can determine its place here by use of the Vasuh (Tengu) language.

Quf can be defined in the Tengu language as follows, Q (Zhee-Nzu) + U (Aum-Zhee) + F (Phe). This sum of the "Quf" equation is Hmu-Hmu. Hmu, in the language of the Tengu, is a letter of sexual energy. Since the term is doubled, we see that there are two sources of this sexual energy merging as one. This means that in this case, Quf is equal to two distinct factions coming together and producing the "egg" found in the Nihongi, or the point of singularity, which creation all stemmed from. This too is in agreement with modern scientific thought. *A Brief Introduction to the Ekpyrotic Universe* by Paul J. Steinhardt, states the following:

"The model is based on the idea that our hot big bang universe was created from the collision of two three-dimensional worlds moving along a hidden, extra dimension. The two three-dimensional worlds collide and "stick," the kinetic energy in the collision is converted the quarks, electrons, photons, etc., that are confined to move along three dimensions. The resulting temperature is finite, so the hot big bang phase begins without a singularity. The universe is homogeneous because the collision and initiation of the big bang phase occurs nearly simultaneously everywhere. The energetically preferred geometry for the two worlds is flat, so their collision produces a flat big bang universe. According to Einstein's equations, this means that the total energy density of the Universe is equal to the critical density. Massive magnetic monopoles, which are overabundantly produced in the standard big bang theory, are not produced at all in this scenario because the temperature after collision is far too small to produce any of these massive particles."

Steinhardt discusses the collision of two three-dimensional worlds, as being the source of the Big Bang, whereas in Shinto, and the much older Ninzuwu form, this "cause" was intentional and involved a "sexual" energy of some cosmic level. Later, in the Ivory Tablets of the Crow, we also discover the purpose of such:

"The fiery ones built great cities inside the stars that shine in the Land of Shadows."

In the same manner that human beings have advanced to the point where technology seems to make the impossible seem possible, the creation of our universe brings with it a continuation of certain intelligences, in lack of a better word, whose existence is found outside the world of time as we know it. In other words, when life in higher dimensions reproduces itself, that which is being reproduced, develops in the third dimension. The "Quf," which equates in the language of the Ninzuwu as Hmu-Hmu verifies this.

Hmu-Hmu equals Lewhu, which means "starry initiation." The Ivory Tablets of the Crow reveal to us that the purpose of all life is its initiation. It states:

"For initiation is the only law that is just unto man."

This was purposely created by the fourth-dimensional race of man in efforts of extending the existence of the fourth and higher dimensions itself. This may seem obscure to some of our readers, so let's expand on this topic further.

Earlier, we mentioned that our use of technology has made life more convenient, even the miraculous seems possible. Just imagine what human beings could do if they had total use of their brain and today's technology as a starting point in 20,000 years. Now imagine what the fourth and higher dimensional races of men could do, they technology they presently possess. The reason why mankind has not come to these truths is expressed for us in the Ivory Tablets of the Crow:

"Thus, the journey begins with a circle…With a circle the journey never ends…This is the question of man…For he will never understand the answer."

The passage cited above has many meanings, but one in particular that I find fascinating is that the world in time can only understand its cause of existence by entering the world outside of time. The Ivory Tablets of the Crow mentions the following:

"Know that every civilization comes into this world in the manner of the Unborn. Each city exists in a place not known to time and then descends upon the realm of man as a kingdom, through some act of war, or a great migration. Do not worship these things like men do, for it is a forbidden art which keeps the soul bound to useless things."

The higher dimensions of man, make up what is known as the world of the future. Reincarnation, in the true sense of the term, means that one goes back. The term "re" means to *go back*. When we reincarnate, we are traveling from the future into the past. The three-dimensional world exists in time, but more importantly, in comparison to the fourth dimensional world and higher realms, the third dimension actually exists in the past. Life in this universe has "reincarnated" or descended from the world of the future (the 4th dimensional plane) into the past in order to advance this world and perpetuate continued existence.

The realms beyond the third dimension are not accessible to the man of the three-dimensional world, using only his five senses. This does not mean that these planes of existence are fantasy, but they can be accessed by those who have developed additional senses of perception beyond those of the three-dimensional plane. Our thoughts, feelings, and emotions are not detectable by the five senses, but they are real indeed. Plants cannot see us the way we see them, yet they can discern our thoughts.

The fourth dimension, accessible by extra-sensory perception, has as its foundation the divine quality of love. Matter of the fourth dimension is love. However, it should also be noted that this quality of divine love, existing in the fourth and higher dimensions, originates in a place that is not relative to the five senses. When humans think of love, it is in association with certain imagery that doesn't exist on these higher planes of being and is therefore not the quality of divine love as defined by man. It is due to such that, the celestial bodies cast upon the world of humanity, and individually, certain challenges, that serves as initiations for us to develop a small glimpse of this multi-universal quality. With the expansion of our universe comes more lessons in extra-stellar initiations for the three-dimensional man with the being the same as his future.

The Art of Ninzuwu is a practice used to revitalize the spirit and awaken it. In the Ivory Tablets of the Crow, we read:

"Know that the Workers of the Miraculous Arts in the world before saw these things in parable, and gave each feeling a name, thereby binding it to a particular function. It was then that the spirit was free to rise up back to its throne again."

In order to facilitate this process, the Initiate makes use of certain letters, known only as the Vasuh. What is the origin of this language?

The Origin of Vasuh

Since the release of the Ivory Tablets of the Crow, the Vasuh language has been a subject of much controversy. It is believed by some to be the language of the Ninzuwu. In the introduction of the Ivory Tablets of the Crow, we read:

"The fourth tablet is entitled The Sword of the Ninzuwu. The Ninzuwu appear to be adepts whose bodies are made out of dark matter, and exist in a world before time. The Cult of Nyarzir implemented methods so that one could evolve to a state of being as that of the Ninzuwu."

Based on what is written in the Ivory Tablets of the Crow, the Ninzuwu appear to be inter-dimensional beings, those existing in the future world, the world of now. Later, in the Ivory Tablets introduction, it states:

"The next tablet is entitled *The Nine Books of Dreams*, wherein nine glyphs of what is known as the Vasuh script are given. These characters represented "shadow chakras," which allowed one to access a universe of dark matter when put into certain formula."

Here it can be clearly seen that the Vasuh language is an esoteric one, for it relates to the "shadow chakras." These shadow chakras are popularly known as back-side chakras. Shadow chakras relate to the unconscious self. It is by our work with the "unconscious" side of ourselves that we become aware of the unseen causes of visible realities. We also become aware of the language of intuition, which is how communication exists within nature.

The term Vasuh, is identical in pronunciation to the term Vasu. Wikipedia defines Vasu as follows:

"In Hinduism, the Vasus are attendant deities of Indra, and later Vishnu. They are eight elemental gods (called "Aṣṭa-vasu", 'Eight Vasus') representing aspects of nature, representing cosmic natural phenomenon. The name Vasu means 'Dweller' or 'Dwelling'."

If the Vasuh is indeed the same as the term Vasu, then we can say that it is the language of phenomena, as Vasu represents "cosmic natural phenomena." Indra is known as the Lord of Heaven in many branches of Hinduism. His symbol is the lightning, as he is a storm god. This is interesting, for we are told the following in the Ivory Tablets of the Crow:

"Nine books in the Dream...Like a lightning bolt..It binds what is Self..To that which is Self."

The term Vasu also relates to the Indian deity named Vasuki. In a book entitled, *The Ruling Races of Prehistoric Times in India*, by James Francis Katherinus Hewitt, we read:

"This god Vasu, the Indian snake-god Vasuki was originally the Northern spring-god,"

Vasuki is a naga, one of the serpents of Hindu and Buddhist mythology. He is a great king of the nagas and has a gem (Nagamani) on his head. Nagas are often depicted as cobras and serpents. In a book written by Amira El-Zein, entitled, *Islam, Arabs, and the Intelligent World of the Jinn*, we read:

"Indian myths speak also of a battle that occurred at a certain point in time between the god Indra and a gigantic serpent that entrapped the waters and kept them from gushing. Indra defeated it, though, and made the waters stream again. By killing the serpent, the god mastered the powers of chaos that threatened to destroy the world, and reinstated order. The serpent was also believed to be a cosmic force, like the kundalini, which is a feminine noun meaning serpent. Kundalini is essential spiritual energy pictured as a twisting serpent slumbering in each of us."

Another text that gives us a deeper meaning of the term naga, is *Out of Isolation* by Frans Welman, where we read:

"Though ideas of a Supreme Creator and afterlife did exist, traditional Nagas believed in the forces of nature and were as animists. For us the natural world is alive with invisible forces, spirits."

Here we see on one hand that the term Naga can represent a cosmic force, while on another represented an ancient people who shared in a magical relationship with the world of nature.

We can find answers as to how all of this relates to the Vasuh language in the Ivory tablets of the Crow, and its origin, by investigating something that is said in another Ninzuwu text entitled the Yi Jing Apocrypha of Genghis Khan. In the book's introduction it states:

"Surprisingly, the Art of Ninzuwu didn't originate in ancient Mesopotamia, but in Asia. According to a certain history held by secret societies that practiced the Art of Ninzuwu. The Cult of Nyarzir began in the days of the legendary empire known as Mu. According to the history of Nyarzir, this was an empire that stretched from the Pacific Ocean and into the regions of what is known today as ancient Mesopotamia. Later, after the time of the deluge, the Empire of Mu fell and its residents divided themselves up into nations. It is also said in these oral traditions of the Ninzuwu that the Yi Jing was formulated during the time that this empire flourished."

According to the Yi Jing Apocrypha of Genghis Khan, the Art of Ninzuwu originated in Asia. This would also mean the same for its language. In the book The Lost Continent of Mu, by James Churchward, we find the authors account of how he came to know of a secret knowledge and language that at one time ruled Asia:

"For more than two years I studied diligently a dead language my priestly friend believed to be the original tongue of mankind. He informed me that this language was understood by only two other high priests in India. A great difficulty arose from the fact that many of the apparently simple inscriptions had hidden meanings which had been designed especially for the Holy Brothers — the Naacals a priestly brotherhood sent from the motherland to the colonies to teach the sacred writings, religion and the sciences… In discussing these secret writings he added something that sent my curiosity up to a new high point. He had already mentioned the legendary Motherland of Man— the mysterious land of Mu. Now he amazed me by the admission that the precious tablets were believed by many to have been written by the Naacals,"

While some modern scholars seek to discredit Churchward's research into lost continent of Mu, he was a patented inventor. While science has long since disproven Churchward's claims, he did set in motion a model of an empire known as Mu that existed in ancient times. Wikipedia states the following in this regard:

"Churchward claimed to have gained his knowledge of the Naacals after befriending an <u>Indian</u> priest, who taught him to read the ancient dead language of the Naacals, spoken by only three people in all of India. The priest disclosed the existence of several ancient tablets, written by the Naacals, and Churchward gained access to these records after overcoming the priest's initial reluctance. His knowledge remained incomplete, as the available tablets were mere fragments of a larger text, but Churchward claimed to have found verification and further information in the records of other ancient peoples."

This description of Churchward's work is very similar to the Ninzuwu, as described in the Ivory Tablets:

"..The Cult of Nyarzir inscribed the knowledge of their mystical tradition on fifteen tablets of ivory that they called "The Crow." The Ivory Tablets describe what seems to be an initiatory journey into what is known today as *pure consciousness*."

In the book sacred Symbols of Mu, by James Churchward, we read:

"They tell us that a body of trained masters from Mu, called Naacals, were carrying to her various colonies and colonial empires copies of the Motherland's Sacred Inspired Religion. These Naacals formed in each country colleges for the teaching of the priestcraft religion, and the sciences. The priesthoods that were formed in these colleges in turn taught the people. There is a very interesting ancient writing about the Chaldis, as the colleges were called in Babylonia. It says: "Everyone was welcome, be he prince or slave. Directly they passed into the temple, they were equal, for they stood in the presence of the Heavenly Father, the Father of them all, and here they became brothers in fact. No payment was charged; all was free..... "The school of the ancient gynosophists was still subsisting in the great city of Benares on the banks of the Ganges. There the Brahmins cultivated the *Sacred Language* which they called *Hanferit*, and look upon it as the most ancient of all languages. [The Naacal writings are in what is here called Hanferit.]

"They admit of Genii, like the primitive Persians. They *tell* their *disciples* that symbols are made only to fix the attention of the people and are different *emblems* of the Deity. But as this sound theology *would turn to no profit*, they concealed it from the people. [And taught what produced superstitious awe and fear.]"

The Vasuh language is the ancient language of the Mu. Different than Churchward's essay, Mu was an empire that reached from Mesopotamia to Japan. This is discussed in great detail in the Yi Jing Apocrypha of Genghis Khan. The supernatural race of beings called the Naacals, and later the Naga, are the Ninzuwu. The legend of the continent Mu sinking may have begun from an actual cataclysm in the area of the Pacific Ocean, but esoterically it represents the disappearance of a visible fourth-dimensional influencing man's early history.

Within many of Asia's spiritual paradigms we find evidence of Mu's existence. Korean shamanism is called Mugyo, which literally means "the religion of Mu." We also find many references in the esoteric teachings of Shinto. Yoshikazu Okada, founder of Mahikari, taught that Japan forms the last surviving portion of this continent, once the home of a superb, sun-worshipping culture. These ideas were taught by many Sect Shinto groups and some Shinto Priests. Recently, archeologists have discovered pyramid structures off the coast of Japan. It is possible that this discovery may lead to further evidence about the ancient Empire of Mu.

There is something unique about the Shinto faith. Many of the gods in Shinto mythology are depicted as "serpents," who can shift in appearance and take on human form. It is one of the few, if not the only surviving belief that venerates the sun as a goddess. The Sumerian deities were said to originate in what appears to be Japan. Dilmun is described very much like an area existing in the vicinity of Japan, which seems to be a reference to the Empire of Mu, located around or in the Pacific Ocean. Michael Rice, in a book entitled, *Egypt's Making: The Origins of Ancient Egypt 5000-2000 BCE*, states:

"In Sumerian texts which celebrate Dilmun various epithets are customarily attached to it, by which it is represented as a paradisial place where the gods dwelt and in which numerous act of creation took place. It is called the Land of Crossing, the Land where the Sun Rises (for the Land is situated in the Sea of the Rising Sun) and throughout its literature particular emphasis is placed on Dilmun's purity,.."

One amazing thing about Shinto spirituality is its consistency with science. It is best known as a spiritual technology. In the Yi Jing Apocrypha of Genghis Khan, we read:

"These atmospheric conditions, or atmosphere, are symbolic of water or *mi*. In a previous work entitled, *The Dark Knight of Nyarlathotep*, we find the following under the chapter *True Religion*:

"In the so-called modern world, terms like polytheism seem to denote some sort of primitive form of spirituality, when in fact, it was a synthesis of how to define the subtle energy that permeates throughout all objects and animates all living things. So in ancient times, a body of water, or an ocean, was considered to be a deity. Now the fact that this ocean was considered to be a deity should not be interpreted in the same manner of how Christians worship Jesus, but as a force of influence upon the environment. Other objects of nature were also deified based on their influence over the environment. These forces were scientifically categorized based on how much subtle energy they emitted into the atmosphere and their influence on objects in the surrounding area, which led to its placement in the hierarchy of natural forces.

These forces were recorded in history as pagan gods, making it easy for the layman to understand them. These forces were also measured by the influence they had on the emotional constitution of animals and humans. Since man possessed an abundance of subtle, or life-force energy, he could use this energy to alter the influence of a powerful force by calling its name (vibrational formulae) and speaking to the energy that resonated behind the said object, be it animal, plant, or star. Speech is vibration, and how words and letters are put together affect other objects vibrating on a subtle level. The enunciation of the names of these forces matched their vibrational level, and in turn they responded in favor of man. The subtle force that is radiated by all animated life was known as fire, and the atmosphere was considered to be water."

Understanding the Kami from this perspective redefines Japanese spirituality for the Western mind. A Japanese deity that rules over the auto industry is not some pagan god, but a force of influence upon the modern world. The force that is responsible for automotive technology can be called upon once it is given a name. Calling upon this name will allow Japanese automotive engineers access to the same ideas that led to the invention of the automobile. Thus, after entreating the *emotional energy* or *kami* that is behind the engineering, manufacturing, and technology of the automotive industry, they will be given the knowledge to advance such. Within Shinto lies the understanding of how to manage and curb the emotional energy, the ki energy that radiates from objects, thoughts, and ideas in one's experience, for the personal benefit of all, or that of a village, or the nation at large. This way of thinking was an inherent result of the hunter-gatherer culture of ancient Japan. In pre-historic Japan, it was important for ancient man to have a working relationship with the environment that he lived in."

An image of the Johuta

The Art of Ninzuwu is a form of Shinto spirituality originating during the Jomon Period, when priests and priestesses were in direct communication with the Ninzuwu and other forces of nature.

Zhee Mudra

Vasuh Letter:

Mantra: Izanagi-no-Mikoto, Izanami-no-Mikoto mamori tamae sakihae tamae (6 times)

Power: *The power to tell the reasonable law of cause and effect from an unreasonable one neglecting the causal law.*

Age of the Gods (Nihon Shoki): "Of old, Heaven and Earth were not yet separated, and the In and Yo not yet divided. They formed a chaotic mass like an egg which was of obscurely defined limits and contained germs.

The purer and clearer part was thinly drawn out, and formed Heaven, while the heavier and grosser element settled down and became Earth.

The finer element easily became a united body, but the consolidation of the heavy and gross element was accomplished with difficulty.

Heaven was therefore formed first, and Earth was established subsequently."

Summary: The Zhee mantra (recited six times) and mudra is used to understand the cause of an event or situation. All phenomena in this universe begins with the intercourse of Heaven and Earth, or the putting together of the left and right hands.

Zhee is equal to Hmu-Hmu. (26 + 8 + 5 + 5 = 44) The co-mingling of Heaven and Earth is covered for us in the Ivory Tablets of the Crow:

"Quf agreed with what the fiery ones had spoken concerning the creation of a world that exits in time. He went down to the River of Shadows and dipped his finger in the Egu. With one drop of water he created a dimension that rested between the worlds of death and immortality."

Quf is of the same vibration as Zhee. (17 + 21 + 6 = 44) In an article appearing in the Cult of Nyarzir's blog page, we read:

"In Ninzuwu-Shinto mythology, the creation of this universe was planned by the "fiery ones." Hence they called upon a scientist named "Quf," in order to complete the task. This entity "Quf" has many correspondences in Ninzuwu-Shinto cosmology. We can determine its place here by use of the Vasuh (Tengu) language.

Quf can be defined in the Tengu language as follows, Q (Zhee-Nzu) + U (Aum-Zhee) + F (Phe). This sum of the "Quf" equation is Hmu-Hmu. Hmu, in the language of the Tengu, is a letter of sexual energy. Since the term is doubled, we see that there are two sources of this sexual energy merging as one. In this case, Quf is equal to two distinct factions coming together and producing the "egg" found in the Nihongi, or the point of singularity, which the universe stemmed from. This too, is in agreement with modern scientific thought. A Brief Introduction to the Ekpyrotic Universe by Paul J. Steinhardt, states the following:

"The model is based on the idea that our hot big bang universe was created from the collision of two three-dimensional worlds moving along a hidden, extra dimension. The two three-dimensional worlds collide and "stick," the kinetic energy in the collision is converted the quarks, electrons, photons, etc., that are confined to move along three dimensions. The resulting temperature is finite, so the hot big bang phase begins without a singularity. The universe is homogeneous because the collision and initiation of the big bang phase occurs nearly simultaneously everywhere. The energetically preferred geometry for the two worlds is flat, so their collision produces a flat big bang universe. According to Einstein's equations, this means that the total energy density of the Universe is equal to the critical density. Massive magnetic monopoles, which are over-abundantly produced in the standard big bang theory, are not produced at all in this scenario because the temperature after collision is far too small to produce any of these massive particles."

Steinhardt discusses the collision of two three-dimensional worlds, as being the source of the Big Bang, whereas in Shinto, and the much older Ninzuwu form, this "cause" was intentional and involved a "sexual" energy of some cosmic level. Later, in the Ivory Tablets of the Crow, we also discover the purpose of such:

"The fiery ones built great cities inside the stars that shine in the Land of Shadows."

In the same manner that human beings have advanced to the point where technology seems to make the impossible seem possible, the creation of our universe brings with it a continuation of certain intelligences, in lack of a better word, whose existence is found outside the world of time as we know it. In other words, when life in higher dimensions reproduces itself, that which is being reproduced, develops in the third dimension. The "Quf," which equates in the language of the Ninzuwu as Hmu-Hmu verifies this.

Hmu-Hmu equals Lewhu, which means "starry initiation." The Ivory Tablets of the Crow reveal to us that the purpose of all life is its initiation. It states:

"For initiation is the only law that is just unto man."

This was purposely created by the fourth-dimensional race of man in efforts of extending the existence of the fourth and higher dimensions itself. "

Hmu-Hmu represents the Yin and Yang principles. Through this unification one leaves the world of duality and enters fourth dimensional consciousness. The "Gateway of Fourth Dimensional Consciousness" is held by Izanagi-no-Mikoto and Izanami-no-Mikoto.

Each Vasuh letter represents a parable, star, and universe. In the Vasuh letter Zhee, we see not only the story of the origin of this universe, but also that of Izanagi-no-Mikoto and Izanami-no-Mikoto. Z equals Aum-Phe (26). In this case, Aum-Phe represents *Aum*, which carries the power of the first symbol, and *Phe*, a symbol of the art of levitation and the emotional quality of an object. Aum is invoking the "emotional" quality of the first letter in Phe, the sixth letter. Just what sort of emotional energy is being invoked in this case?

When we add Aum (2) and Phe (6) together, we get Lewhu (8). This reveals to us that it is the emotional quality of the stars that is being invoked, as Lewhu represents the "initiatory aspects of the divine energies of the stars." Here we see that in the first letter of Zhee, Z (Aum-Phe), an emotional attunement to the starry energies takes place. The next letter, H, or Lewhu, which is the eighth letter, does indeed initiate us into understanding the divine language of the stars once we have tuned into its emotional state. Lewhu also represents the use of the Yi Jing, as the number eight is sacred for it represents the foundation, the Bagua.

Following both Z (Aum-Phe), and H (Lewhu), is E, or Bnhu (5). Bnhu represents wealth and the beauty in nature. Bnhu, in the Ivory Tablets of the Crow, is also said to be a teacher of the language of plants. Bnhu also relates to the chakra of the solar plexus. Once again we see another character in the first Vasuh letter, having something to do with the stars. Bnhu (E) represents the drawing down of energy from the stars in process similar to photosynthesis. This energy is used in an appropriate manner. This stellar energy is then returned to its place of origin. Here we see that Bnhu (E) is followed by another Bnhu, showing a process of receive and return. We learn here that the Izanagi-no-Mikoto and Izanami-no-Mikoto represents the use of the seen starry energies and the world of nature. These same energies, when understood, reveals the power to tell the reasonable law of cause and effect (Izanagi-no-Mikoto) from an unreasonable one neglecting the causal law (Izanami-no-Mikoto).

Izanagi-no-Mikoto represents yang energy and Izanami-no-Mikoto represents yin energy. These are the light and dark aspects of the divine sexual energy, the unified Heaven and Earth consciousness of the fourth dimension. Many ancient writings, as in the case of the Mesopotamians, describe a time when the "waters were one." This means a time when the fourth dimensional quality was not separated from earthly man. Before Izanami-no-Mikoto became ruler of the Netherworld, the Land of Yomi, she was united with the Heavens, or Izanagi-no-Mikoto. We read in the Nihon Shoki:

"The Gods of Heaven addressed Izanagi no Mikoto and Izanami no Mikoto, saying: 'There is the country Toyo-ashi-hara-chi-i-wo-aki no midzu-ho. Do ye proceed and bring it to order.' They then gave them the jewel-spear of Heaven. Hereupon the two Gods stood on the floating bridge of Heaven, and plunging down the spear, sought for land. Then upon stirring the ocean with it, and bringing it up again, the brine which dripped from the spear-point coagulated and became an island, which was called Ono-goro-jima. The two gods descended, dwelt in this island, and erected there an eight-fathom palace. They also set up the pillar of Heaven."

It was by the unification of heavenly and earthly forces that the "eight" islands of what is known as Japan today, was produced. In like manner, Zhee is the source of the remaining eight Vasuh letters.

When one invokes the dimension of Zhee they can learn a lot from their invisible journeys that will occur after this rite is called into being. The Initiate will then experience a verification of the Baptism of the Ancient One. Later, they will see the origin and causes of some of the most subtle situations. These dreams are a safe form of trance. It is also an energy that heals and helps us in our personal and romantic relationships.

The Zhee mudra can also be used for meetings between other Initiates. In this case, the focus would be on a particular location, and attendance thereof would take place by visualization after Zhee has been invoked. The members need not do the meditation at the same time for they will find themselves in the same place during their journeys.

The Zhee mudra is a timeless dimension. It is the invocation of our own intuition. Some use this sign before readings. However its main purpose is the spark of the fourth dimensional quality.

The Zhee mudra is the door that enables one access to the fourth dimensional world and beyond. It is written in the Age of the Gods:

"These make eight Deities in all. Being formed by the mutual action of the Heavenly and Earthly principles, they were made male and female. From Kuni no toko-tachi no Mikoto to Izanagi no Mikoto and Izanami no Mikoto are called the seven generations of the age of the Gods."

Aum Mudra

Vasuh Letter:

Mantra: A-ma-te-ra-su-O-ho-mi-ka-mi (6 times)

Power: The ability to know the fourth dimensional quality and send the energy of love to any location in the past, present, or future.

Age of the Gods (Nihon Shoki): **"After this Izanagi no Mikoto and Izanami no Mikoto consulted together, saying:- "We have now produced the Great-island country, with the mountains, rivers, herbs, and trees. Why should we not produce someone who shall be lord of the universe? They then produced the Sun Goddess, who was called Oho-hiru-me no muchi. Called Ama-terasu no Oho kami. In one writing called Ama-terasu-oho-hiru-me no Mikoto. The resplendent lustre of this child shone throughout all the six quarters."**

The Aum mudra is a symbol of Amaterasu-Ohmikami. It is used by the Initiate to send a fourth dimensional quality to any of the "six quarters," which are symbolic of all events and experiences that fall under the domain of the realm of the phenomenal world. Amaterasu-Ohmikami is not only the mantra of our personal Sun, but of the realm of the Suns, described by some in the Ray of Creation teachings. Amaterasu Ohmikami represents the biophotonic process occurring in living things.

The Aum mudra can be used to send the fourth dimensional quality of love to a person, place, and experience that exists in the three dimensional realm. The practitioner would visualize sending this energy to the situation at hand while chanting its mantra. In more intimate settings, the Aum sign, or symbol can be drawn into the client's aura.

The Initiate must call the name *Amaterasu-O-Ohmikami* six times, visualizing the energy filling their own aura and then sending it forward where needed.

Amaterasu Ohmikami, along with her brother, Tsukiyomi-no-Mikoto, rule the workings of the Yi Jing. We are told the following in the Nihon Shoki:

"The resplendent lustre of this child shone throughout all the six quarters. Therefore, the two Deities rejoiced, saying: "We have had many children, but none of them have been equal to this wondrous infant. She ought not to be kept long in this land, but we ought of our own accord to send her at once to Heaven, and entrust to her the affairs of Heaven."

At this time Heaven and Earth were still not far separated, and therefore they sent her up to Heaven by the ladder of Heaven.

They next produced the Moon-god. Called in one writing Tsuki-yumi no Mikoto, or Tsukiyomi no Mikoto.

His radiance was next to that of the Sun in splendor. This God was to be the consort of the Sun-Goddess, and to share in her government. They sent him also to Heaven."

The "six quarters," or hexagram, which Amaterasu Ohmikami had "shone upon," was North, South, East, West, Above, Below, as W. G. Aston points out in a version of the Nihon Shoki. In other words, four spaces above and for spaces below, which would make eight spaces. This "rulership of Heaven" was to be shared with Tsukiyomi-no-Mikoto, producing another eight spaces for the moon. In this case both, Amaterasu Ohmikami and Tsukiyomi-no-Mikoto rule eight spaces, or what is known in Yi Jing terminology as the Bagua. Eight times eight equals sixty-four, the number of hexagrams (six quartered symbols) in the Yi Jing. Based upon such, we can see that it is proper to invoke Amaterasu Ohmikami before Yi Jing readings.

The energy of Amaterasu Ohmikami is invigorating. The sun goddess is a chairman, an ambassador of the "heavenly council." Our Sun receives messages from others stars and shines these fates upon Earth. This can be seen in the Vasuh letter of Aum.

The first letter is Aum is A, or Zhee (1). Zhee, in the Vasuh language, means "light of the goddess." This means that the Sun, Amaterasu Ohmikami is able to visually radiate a force upon which all life on Earth is dependent upon. It also implies that we can gain sight into a situation by having the light of Amaterasu Ohmikami shine upon what is hidden.

The letter in Aum is u, or Aum-Zhee (21). Aum-Zhee not only represents calling on the "light of the goddess," but being able to send such to any distant location. In the Ivory Tablets of the Crow, we read:

"Aum. It is the second letter in the language of Vasuh. It can be used to carry the powers of the first symbol to any distant location. It can also be used to send and read the thoughts of others."

Amaterasu Ohmikami is an ambassador of the fourth dimensional quality. It is for this reason that her symbol is the mirror. The mirror is the invoker of the "light of the goddess." In the Nihon Shoki we read:

"At this time Ama-terasu no Oho-kami took in her hand the precious mirror, and, giving it to Ame no Oshi-ho-mi-mi no Mikoto, uttered a prayer, saying : — ' My child, when thou lookest upon this mirror, let it be as if thou wert looking on me. Let it be with thee on thy couch and in thy hall, and let it be to thee a holy' mirror.'"

One symbol of Amaterasu Ohkami is the mirror. We have an "inner sun goddess," a soul if you will. Our work is to become attuned to our inner vibration. In doing so, we come to realize that our initiation into the Art of Ninzuwu is not about "entering a certain" perspective, but a lifting of the veil and seeing the world already-existing beyond the five senses. The sheds light in dark spaces. It nurtures not just awareness, but awareness of our intuitive power. In the first two letters of Aum, A (Zhee), and U (Aum-Zhee), we see an interplay between the unseen light and the cultivation of our inner being, which absorbs this light.

The next letter, M, in the Vasuh language is Zhee-Tuu. It reflects the "light of the goddess" in the aspect of Tuu, which deals with the manipulation of the vital force. Tuu is relative to Tsukiyomi-no-Mikoto, the Kami of the Moon.

The sign of Amaterasu Ohmi-kami, the Aum mudra, increases vitality and promotes growth with business, family, relationships, and other things regarding life. It is a balancing energy and sees the whole point of view, rather than just a perspective. It is written in the Ivory Tablets of the Crow:

"Beyond the stars, beyond the darkness of the night they dwell. Into the realm of light they reside in stillness. Without need of the elements, for what is it? It is consciousness. The mere reflection of these words caused that which is self-aware to stare at itself in darkness."

The Aum mudra teaches us how to integrate the fourth dimensional quality of love effectively into our lives. Based on what we learn and how, we can then join the ranks of those who work towards the evolution of our three dimensional world.

Tuu Mudra

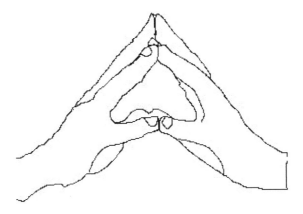

Vasuh Letter: ⽊√

Mantra: Tsukiyomi-no-Mikoto mamori tamae sakihae tamae (6 times)

Power: The ability to keep oneself in the state of enlightenment.

Age of the Gods (Nihon Shoki): "Now when Ama-terasu no Oho-kami was already in Heaven, she said: — 'I hear that in the Central country of reed-plains there is the Deity Uke-mochi no Kami. Do thou, Tsuki-yomi no Mikoto, go and wait upon her.' Tsuki-yomi no Mikoto, on receiving this command, descended and went to the place where Uke-mochi no Kami was. Thereupon Uke-mochi no Kami turned her head towards the land, and forthwith from her mouth there came boiled rice: she faced the sea, and again there came from her mouth things broad of fin and things narrow of fin.

She faced the mountains and again there came from her mouth things rough of hair and things soft of hair. These things were all prepared and set out on one hundred tables for his entertainment. Then Tsuki-yomi no Mikoto became flushed with anger, and said: — 'Filthy! Nasty! That thou shouldst dare to feed me with things disgorged from thy mouth.' So he drew his sword and slew her, and then returned and made his report, relating all the circumstances. Upon this Ama-terasu no Oho-kami was exceedingly angry, and said: — 'Thou art a wicked Deity. I must not see thee face to face.' So they were separated by one day and one night, and dwelt apart."

In the example, cited above, we see a symbolic illustration of Tsukiyomi-no-Mikoto's role during harvest season, an analogy for the moon's influence upon vegetation. Earlier in the Nihon Shoki, we read:

"Now Oho-hirume no Mikoto and Tsuki-yumi no Mikoto were both of a bright and beautiful nature, and were therefore made to shine down upon Heaven and Earth."

Tsuki-yumi no Mikoto rules vitality and also protective. The moon provides light while one is in a state of darkness. The moon radiates an energy that influences the emotional state of animal life and man upon the earth. After one has performed the Baptism of the Ancient One, the energies of the moon strengthens their aura and understanding of the Art of Ninzuwu itself. Tsuki-yomi no Mikoto associated with the Vasuh letter Tuu. In the Ivory Tablets of the Crow, we read:

"Tuu. It is a symbol of protection and increases vitality."

The first letter in the Vasuh Tuu is T (20), or Aum-zero. In the Art of Ninzuwu, zero is always a reflection of what precedes it. This means that Tsuki-yomi-no-Mikoto, the Moon god, reflects the energy of Amaterasu Ohmikami, the Sun goddess. William Aston, in a book entitled, Shinto (The Way of the Gods), states the following concerning Tsuki-yomi-no-Mikoto:

"The usual derivation of his name is from tsuki, moon, and yomi, darkness. It is to be observed, however, that this yomi is often written with a character which implies a derivation from yomu, to reckon, a word which contains the same root as yubi, finger. "Moon-reckoner" is not an inappropriate name for a luminary which is recognized in so countries as a measurer of time. Tsuki-yomi was represented at Ise as a man riding a horse, clad in purple and girt with a golden sword. Another shintai of his was a mirror."

Here we see that Tsuki-yomi carried the "sword" and as associated with the mirror. The mirror is a symbol of the Amaterasu Ohmikami, as the moon reflects her light. The sword is symbol of the stars. After the letter T (Aum-zero), in the Vasuh article Tuu, is followed by U (Aum-Zhee) and another U (Aum-Zhee) This means that and the moon reflects the light of Amaterasu Ohmikami, it is also shining forth that which Amaterasu Ohmikami, the Sun goddess, gains from both Izanagi-no-Mikoto and Izanami-no-Mikoto.

In the first sequence of Aum-Zhee, U (21), the Moon god, Tsuki-yomi-no-Mikoto, absorbs from the Sun goddess an aspect of Izanagi-no-Mikoto, appearing as the full moon. The second sequence of Aum-Zhee, U (21), would then represent, the Moon god, Tsuki-yomi-no-Mikoto, absorbs from the Sun goddess an aspect of Izanami-no-Mikoto, appearing as the new moon. Based on such, we can say that the Vasuh letter Tuu, represents first, Tsuki-yomi-no-Mikoto's reflection of the light of Sun's light, T (Aum-zero). Next, the Moon god's role as full and new moons, attributes absorbed from the Sun's light, but originating in Izanagi-no-Mikoto and Izanami-no-Mikoto, U (Aum-Zhee), U (Aum-Zhee). This is the equation of the Vasuh letter Tuu, is regards to Ninzuwu-Shinto.

The Three Pure Ones of Ninzuwu-Shinto

The Three Pure Ones of Ninzuwu are found in the first three Vasuh letters, Zhee, Aum, and Tuu. These three Vasuh letters also correspond to mudras, which are discussed here in this text. The first three mudras represent the following:

Zhee = Izanagi-no-Mikoto and Izanami-no-Mikoto = Realm of Black and White Holes

Aum = Amaterasu Ohmikami = Realm of Suns, Realm of Light, also Stars.

Tuu = Tsuki-yomi-no-Mikoto = Realm of the Planets and Satellites.

The ways of the Three Pure Ones is perfect and just, for they reveal the code of universal order. Let us take a look at these three Vasuh letters more closely.

Znee = z (26) + h (8) + e (5) + e (5) = 44 = 4 + 4 = 8. The final sum of Zhee is 8.
Aum = a (1) + u (21) + m (13) = 35 = 3 + 5 = 8. The final sum of Aum is 8.
Tuu = t (20) + u (21) + u (21) = 62 = 6 + 2 = 8. The final sum of Tuu is 8.

Based on the equations presented above, the first three Vasuh letters possess the same value of eight. Eight is a sacred number in Shinto spirituality. *Shinto: A Celebration of Life*, written by Aiden Rankin states:

"Eight is a sacred number in Shinto, containing in it the connotation of infinity and associated with the life force."

On page 571, of a book entitled, *The I Ching in the Shinto Thought of Tokugawa, Japan*, we read:

"The most striking similarity between the I Ching and Shinto, he believed, was that they both favored the number eight, which reflected the universality of the divine way of heaven and earth:

The Chinese sage, Fu Hsi, was the first to draw the lines of ch'ien and k'un, which were later developed into the six lines, the eight trigrams, and [eight times eight to produce] the sixty-four hexagrams. Similarly, we [Japanese] used the number eight in words, such as the Yatano [Mirror] and the Yasaka [Jade], because the divine way of heaven and earth is one, and it is naturally the same wonderful principle shared by both Japan and China."

There are many instances where the number "eight" appears in Shinto mythology. Eight represents the Way of Heaven and Earth in its perfection. Based on such, the first three Vasuh letters represent this perfection of Heaven and Earth in the respective dimensions that each of these three powers represent. We are told the following in the Nihon Shoki:

"Now Oho-hirume no Mikoto and Tsuki-yumi no Mikoto were both of a bright and beautiful nature, and were therefore made to shine down upon Heaven and Earth."

The rotation, the interchange between these respective dimensions of Zhee, Aum, and Tuu, creates what is known as "the sea." In the ancient mythologies of several nations, we find that the "sea" means the atmosphere, and dimension. This can even be seen in the Babylonian Creation epic, where we read:

"When the skies above were not yet named
Nor earth below pronounced by name,
Apsu, the first one, their begetter,
And maker Tiamat, who bore them all,
Had mixed their waters together,
But had not formed pastures, nor discovered reed-beds;
When yet no gods were manifest,
Nor names pronounced, nor destinies decreed,
Then gods were born within them."

Seventy-percent of the Earth is covered by water. Water is one of the most influential forces here on Earth. It not only reflects the cosmic energies of the Sun and Moon, but it also stands as a body of its own, as it contains various forms of life, in the same way that the human body is a host to cell, germs and etc.

Interestingly, in the Yi Jing Apocrypha of Genghis Khan, all the Ninzuwu dreams appear in the realms of the trigram for water. The term Vasuh, is related to Vasu, another name for the Naga King Vasuki. The Naga kings were later revered in China and Japan as dragons. *The Dragon in China and Japan*, written by M. W. Di Visser, states:

"As we have seen above, the Indian Naga legends served already in the time of the Nihongi, i. e. in the beginning of the eighth century, to embellish the old tales concerning the Japanese sea-gods....It is no wonder then, that the more Buddha's Law flourished in Japan, the more the original Japanese sea and river-gods had to give way to the Indian conquerors; therefore most of the dragons, mentioned in later works, are Nagas."

Initiation into the realm of the "dragon" was extremely important in ancient times. In the Secret Doctrine by H. P. Blavatsky, Volume 1, we read:

"For instance, when Philostratus narrates that the natives of India and Arabia fed on the heart and liver of serpents in order to learn the language of all the animals, the serpent being credited with that faculty, he certainly never meant his words to be accepted literally. (See *De Vita Apollonii*, lib. 1, c. xiv.) As will be found more than once as we proceed, the "Serpent" and "Dragon" were the names given to the "Wise Ones," the initiated adepts of olden times. It was their wisdom and their learning that were devoured or assimilated by their followers, whence the allegory. When the Scandinavian Sigurd is fabled to have roasted the heart of Fafnir, the Dragon, whom he had slain, becoming thereby the wisest of men, it meant the same thing. Sigurd had become learned in the runes and magical charms; he had received the "word" from an initiate of that name, or from a sorcerer, after which the latter died, as many do, after "passing the word." Epiphanius lets out a secret of the Gnostics while trying to expose their *heresies*. The Gnostic Ophites, he says, had a reason for honouring the Serpent: *it was because he taught the primeval men the Mysteries* (*Adv. Haeres.* 37). Verily so; but they did not have Adam and Eve in the garden in their minds when teaching this dogma, but simply that which is stated above. The *Nagas* of the Hindu and Tibetan adepts were human *Nagas* (Serpents), not reptiles. Moreover, the Serpent has ever been the type of consecutive or serial rejuvenation, of IMMORTALITY and TIME."

The Nagas, or Dragons, were human adepts and keepers of a sacred knowledge. In Asian mythology, the dragons are symbolically depicted as living in the bottom of the ocean, a symbol of the invisible realm that these adepts took upon permanent residence in after no longer needing the mortal body. These Nagas, Dragons, and Tengu, represented various schools of high esoteric knowledge that is hidden and will only be revealed to those who are sincere in a particular working, and it must be noted that all of these, are in themselves, names coined by the layman for the Ninzuwu.

The Ninzuwu is a term used not only for the human adepts of ancient times, who were able to pass between realms and other dimensions, but those that labor behind the veil. Some of these have never been confined to the worlds of time and space. It is a kingdom that has no beginning and has never come to pass. In the Ivory Tablets of the Crow, we read concerning the Sword of Ninzuwu:

"Know that every civilization comes into this world in the manner of the Unborn. Each city exists in a place not known to time and then descends upon the realm of man as a kingdom, through some act of war, or a great migration. Do not worship these things like men do, for it is a forbidden art which keeps the soul bound to useless things."

According to the Ivory Tablets of the Crow, each civilization appearing on earth is an actual incarnation of a heavenly kingdom. The Ivory Tablets assertion of the worship of the earthly kingdom because it is in a decadent state. However, the Initiate can visit the heavenly aspect of these kingdoms with the formulas given in this text. The point here is that behind the veil of the phenomenal world is a glorious kingdom where much of the deities depicted in ancient lore are united, and those of this kingdom the Initiate can discern by the preliminary workings of The Crow.

Hmu Mudra

Vasuh Letter: ℒ

Mantra: Toyotama-hime-no-Mikoto mamori tamae sakihae tamae (8 times)

Power: The gift of enchantment and the ability to see and sense things not visible to ordinary man. It also can be used to heal eyesight and in opening the gate, allowing one to walk among the Ninzuwu.

Age of the Gods (Nihon Shoki): **"Hoho-demi no Mikoto, sank it in the sea. Forthwith he found himself at a pleasant strand, where he abandoned the basket, and, proceeding on his way, suddenly arrived at the palace of the Sea-God. This palace was provided with battlements and turrets, and had stately towers. Before the gate there was a well, and over the well there grew a many-branched cassia-tree, with wide-spreading boughs and leaves. Now Hiko-hoho-demi no Mikoto went up to the foot of this tree and loitered about. After some time a beautiful woman appeared, and, pushing open the door, came forth. She at length took a jewel-vessel and approached. She was about to draw water, when, raising her eyes, she saw him, and was alarmed. Returning within, she spoke to her father and mother, saying: — 'There is a rare stranger at the foot of the tree before the gate." The God of the Sea thereupon prepared an eight-fold cushion and led him in. When they had taken their seats, he inquired of him the object of his coming. Then Hiko-hoho-demi no Mikoto explained to him in reply all the circumstances. After this, Hiko-hoho-demi no Mikoto took to wife the Sea-God's daughter, Toyo-tama-hime, and dwelt in the sea-palace."**

Hikohohodemi-no-Mikoto is also known in some accounts as Hoori. His account also appears in the *Yi Jing Apocrypha of Genghis Khan*. The legend of Hoori gives us insight into *the power of Toyotama-hime-no-Mikoto*. In a Wikipedia article, under the title Hoori, we read:

"Hoori's legend is told in both the Kojiki and the Nihon shoki. Hoori was a hunter, and he had an argument with his brother Hoderi, a fisherman, over a fish-hook that Hoori had forced his elder brother to lend him and had lost. Hoderi claimed that Hoori should give back the fish-hook, for he

refused to accept another one (due to the belief that each tool is animated and hence unique). Hoori then descended to the bottom of the sea to search, but was unable to find it. Instead, he found Toyotama-hime (Princess Toyotama), also known as Otohime, the daughter of the sea god, Ryūjin. The sea god helped Hoori find Hoderi's lost hook, and Hoori later married the sea god's daughter Toyotamahime."

Toyotama-hime-no-Mikoto is the daughter of the sea god Ryujin, also known as O-Watatsumi. Toyotama-hime means luminous jewel, the symbolism of which we will later discuss. Her father, O-Watatsumi, was known to bestow the "tide jewels" of Shinto myth, upon those whom he favored. This was the case with Hikohohodemi-no-Mikoto, also known as Hoori. O-Watatsumi gave the "tide Jewels," or wish-fulfilling jewels, to his son-in-law Hoori, in hopes that it would help him resolve his conflict with his brother. In the Nihon Shoki, we read:

"He further presented to him the jewel of the flowing tide and the jewel of the ebbing tide, and instructed him, saying: "If thou dost dip the tide-flowing jewel, the tide will suddenly flow, and there-withal thou shalt drown thine elder brother. But in case thy elder brother should repent and beg forgiveness, if, on the contrary', thou dip the tide-ebbing jewel, the tide will spontaneously ebb, and therewithal thou shalt save him. If thou harass him in this way, thy elder brother will of his own accord render submission."

The first letter of the Vasuh power Hmu is H (8), or Lewhu. Toyatama-hime-no-Mikoto is an energy that also opens the path of initiation into the deeper mysteries of mysticism and the occult. In the Nihon Shoki's account of Hikohohodemi-no-Mikoto, cited earlier, we read:

"…proceeding on his way, suddenly arrived at the palace of the Sea-God. This palace was provided with battlements and turrets, and had stately towers. Before the gate there was a well, and over the well there grew a many-branched cassia-tree, with wide-spreading boughs and leaves. Now Hiko-hoho-demi no Mikoto went up to the foot of this tree and loitered about. After some time a beautiful woman appeared, and, pushing open the door, came forth. She at length took a jewel-vessel and approached. She was about to draw water, when, raising her eyes, she saw him, and was alarmed. Returning within, she spoke to her father and mother, saying: — 'There is a rare stranger at the foot of the tree before the gate."

Based on this description, we can see that "the palace of the Sea-God," was not literally underwater, as there stood a "many-branched cassia-tree" outside of its gate. Also we find in the account that the daughter of the Sea-God went outside the palace, seeking to draw water from a well. This clearly shows that the "sea" is indeed a metaphor for a realm, or another dimension.

The next letter in the Vasuh Hmu is M (Zhee-Tuu), or 13. Zhee-Tuu relates to the moon cycles. Zhee is the light and shadow energies of Izanagi-no-Mikoto and Izanami-no-Mikoto reflected in Tuu, Tsuki-yomi-no-Mikoto, the Vasuh power Tuu, kami of the Moon in its full and new moon phases. Therefore, the initiation rites of the sea is a lunar alchemy, as the Moon has influence over the Sea.

The next letter in Hmu is U (21), or Aum-Zhee. While Aum-Zhee would normally represent the power that the Sun Goddess absorbs from the stellar black and white wholes in space, symbolic of Izanagi-no-Mikoto and Izanami-no-Mikoto. (Black holes rotate. On one side they appear to be black, functioning in a yin aspect. Yet, there is a luminous side of the black hole, a white hole that radiates energy for so many years. These are called white holes.) In this case, however, Aum-Zhee follows Zhee-Tuu (M), which means it is a symbol of the full moon. Aum-Zhee is 21. 2 + 1 = 3, or Tuu, Tsukiyomi-no-Mikoto. In one account, recorded in the Nihon Shoki, Toyatama-hime discovers Hikohohodemi-no-Mikoto, due to his reflection in the well, which reveals a certain formula of ritual and the presence of a strong luminary.

Toyatama-hime-no-Mikoto is the Gatekeeper of a very rare and sacred knowledge. She is the guardian of deep occult mysteries and a knowledge not known to ordinary man. This can be seen in the legendary account of Hoori itself. Let us review this with a closer eye:

"Before the gate there was a well, and over the well there grew a many-branched cassia-tree, with wide-spreading boughs and leaves. Now Hiko-hoho-demi no Mikoto went up to the foot of this tree and loitered about."

Hikohohodemi-no-Mikoto is said to have stayed at the foot of the many-"branched cassia-tree." Published in in 1885, written by Rev. Timothy Harley, in his examination of superstitions surrounding reverence for the moon, the book, Moon Lore, states:

"On another page of the same work we read: "During the T'ang dynasty it was recounted that a cassia tree grows in the moon, this notion being derived apparently from an Indian source. The *sal* tree (*shorea robusta*), one of the sacred trees of the Buddhists, was said during the Sung dynasty to be identical with the cassia tree in the moon. The lunar hare is said to squat at the foot of the cassia tree, pounding its drugs for the genii. The cassia tree in the moon is said to be especially visible at mid-autumn, and hence to take a degree at the examinations which are held at this period is described as plucking a leaf from the cassia."

Harley's work helps us to see that the presence of the "cassia-tree" in the myth of Hikohohodemi-no-Mikoto pertains to some form of lunar alchemy. Hikohohodemi-no-Mikoto is said to have stood at the foot of the cassia-tree. In the Art of Ninzuwu teachings a tree is relative to the Dream of the Fahmu, where we are told:

"Know too, that the Fahmu often take the nature of trees,"

The term Fahmu consists of *fa* and *hmu*. Fa is symbolic of a vessel for divine energy, and hmu, the realm of the luminous jewel, Toyatama-hime-no-Mikoto. The sum of Fahmu equals 49, which equals 4 + 9 =13, 1 +3 = 4, or Hmu. Based on such, we can definitely see that Hikohohodemi-no-Mikoto was engaged in the mystical practice of the Fahmu and also the Opening of the Sea ceremony.

"After some time a beautiful woman appeared, and, pushing open the door, came forth. She at length took a jewel-vessel and approached. She was about to draw water, when, raising her eyes, she saw him, and was alarmed. Returning within, she spoke to her father and mother, saying: — 'There is a rare stranger at the foot of the tree before the gate."

Toyotama-hime-no-Mikoto protects sacred knowledge from the profane. In our initiation into the Dream of Fahmu, we learned how to communicate with plants and trees. Part of the reason for this exercise is to help the Initiate understand that plants and trees will shut down in their communication with entities that express "negative emotions," and the importance of keeping a positive mind space. This has been observed scientifically. In like manner, the divine world responds the same. No one can enter the divine world if their intent is not in accord with the ways of Heaven and Earth. All this nonsense being propagated by pseudo-occult schools of thought and re-gentrified philosophies that were once labeled as "racist," used in the genocide of millions of innocent people, "might is right," are not the sources of "power" they claim to be, but hold intercourse with the shadow elements and are useful only to those who are dysfunctionally-fascinated with disincarnate spirits. One must cultivate love as a prerequisite in their obtainment of divine knowledge. This is the test of initiation within each and every step of the Divine World.

Toyotama-hime-no-Mikoto, the luminous jewel, helps us to cultivate such love and understand the difference between the definition of love, as often it is held in world-thought, and its true meaning in the Divine World. It is for this reason that we find Toyotama-hime-no-Mikoto aligned with the heart chakra, and the Vasuh letter Hmu.

Bnhu Mudra

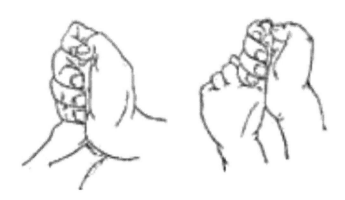

Vasuh Letter: ᛒ

Mantra: Ryu-gu-jo, Oho-Watatsumi-no-Mikoto mamori tamae sakihae tamae (8 times)

Power: The ability to communicate and hold satisfying relationships with plants, trees, and other forms of natural life. Control of Space and Time

Age of the Gods (Nihon Shoki): "After this, Hiko-hoho-demi no Mikoto took to wife the Sea god's daughter, Toyo-tama-hime, and dwelt in the sea-palace. For three years he enjoyed peace and pleasure, but still had a longing for his own country, and therefore sighed deeply from time to time. Toyo-tama-hime heard this and told her father, saying: "The Heavenly Grandchild often sighs as if in grief. It may be that it is the sorrow of long in, for his country. "The god of the Sea thereupon drew to him Hiko-hoho-demi no Mikoto, and addressing him in an easy, familiar way, said: "If the Heavenly Grandchild desires to return to his country I will send him back." So he gave him the fish-hook which he had found, and in doing so instructed him, saying: "When thou givest this fish-hook to thy elder brother, before giving it to him call to it secretly, and say, 'A poor hook.'" He further presented to him the jewel of the flowing tide and the jewel of the ebbing tide, and instructed him, saying: "If thou dost dip the tide-flowing jewel, the tide will suddenly flow, and therewithal thou shalt drown thine elder brother. But in case thy elder brother should repent and beg forgiveness, if, on the contrary, thou dip the tide-ebbing jewel, the tide will spontaneously ebb, and therewithal thou shalt save him. If thou harass him in this way, thy elder brother will of his own accord render submission."

Oho-Watatsumi-no-Mikoto, based on the legend, is a very giving and loving force. In the myth, cited above, he allowed Hikohohodemi-no-Mikoto to marry his daughter. He was able to retrieve the lost fish-hook of Hikohohodemi-no-Mikoto's brother. Additionally, he bestowed the "tide jewels," the wish-fulfilling jewels, upon Hikohohodemi-no-Mikoto. Oho-Watatsumi-no-Mikoto is known as Ryujin.

The sea represents an internal alchemy. The sea is home to various different types of living creatures. In like manner the human body is host to different organs and etc. Based on such wee can say that the sea is a living orgasm, filled with many things just like our bodies are filled with different cells. Oho-

Watatsumi –no-Mikoto teaches how to integrate the outer forces of the moon, sun, and outer heavens into our sea, our experience, and more importantly, our psychology.

The Vasuh power Bnhu, begins with B, or Aum. Aum would represent the power of Amaterasu Ohmikami, the Sun, or realm of stars. Aum in this case, would be symbolic of Toyotama-hime-no-Mikoto, the luminous jewel, being given into marriage to Hikohohodemi-no-Mikoto. This is followed by N, or Zhee-Hmu. Both *Zhee* and *Hmu* are invisible powers of influence. This would mean that in the first two letters of the Vasuh power Bnhu, we find a working of the hidden sun, or inner sun. This aspect of the myth was symbolized by Oho-Watatsumi-no-Mikoto's ability to return the fish-hook to Hikohohodemi-no-Mikoto. It means acquiring what was once lost in ourselves.

The next letter we must consider in Bnhu is H, or Lewhu. Lewhu represents, according to the Ivory Tablets of the Crow, initiatory energies of the stars. We read in the Ivory Tablets:

"It is used in initiating one to the divine energies of the stars."

So far in our equation, we see the divine energy of the stars working with our inner being. This signifies the development of the soul through the starry energies and ability to manipulate the very same power of these stars. In the myth, this is represented by Oho-Watatsumi-no-Mikoto giving Hikohohodemi-no-Mikoto the "tide Jewels."

The final aspect of the Vasuh power Bnhu, gives us a deeper insight into this mysterious working. The final letter of the Vasuh power Bnhu is U, or Aum-Zhee (21). We mentioned before how this relates to the moon. In this case, Aum-Zhee is a symbol of the new moon, as it follows Lewhu. The energies of the stars are more apparent during the dark moon. In this we discover what exactly this mysterious rite is.

In the first part of the myth, concerning Hikohohodemi-no-Mikoto, we find that he drew near the region of the Sea-Deity, during the full moon. The presence of a cassia-tree in the myth confirms this. Later, when Hikohohodemi-no-Mikoto met Oho-Watatsumi-no-Mikoto, he received the "tide jewels," which are symbolic of the ability to harness and control stellar forces, a rite occurring on the new moon.

The presence of the "dark moon" allows one to focus on a zodiac constellation. The Initiate is to enter the different chambers of Ryu-gu-jo (Dragon Palace) every new moon. The Dragon Palace is the zodiac. The idea of a witch's coven meeting in a secret place has a lot to do with this. The same also for Freemasons. Originally, these secret meeting represented the ability to have intercourse with the very same zodiac constellation that the Sun entered. It was considered to be a sacred part of following the Way of Heaven and Earth. We know for certain that Ryugujo relates to the zodiac based on its description. Wikipedia writes under the topic Ryugujo:

"The undersea palace of Ryūjin, the dragon god of the sea. Depending on the version of the legend, it is built from red and white coral, or from solid crystal. The inhabitants of the palace were Ryūjin's families and servants, who were denizens of the sea. In some legends, on *each of the four sides of the palace it is a different season*, and one day in the palace is equal to a century outside its boundaries."

The instruction for entering the zodiac rooms of Ryugujo is given later in this writing. We are told the following in the Ivory Tablets of the Crow:

"The Dream will enter the mind of the Initiate as the waters upon the shore. It is a Dream of Water, for all are born out of Water, even Dreams."

Oho-Watatsumi-no-Mikoto plays a big part in out initiatory process. All of the initiatory Dreams mentioned in the Ivory Tablets of the Crow are described in his realm in the Yi Jing Apocrypha of Genghis Khan.

Phe Mudra

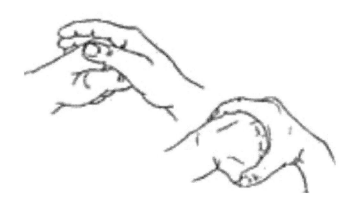

Vasuh Letter: 𝕌𝓱

Mantra: Tamayori-hime-no-Mikoto mamori tamae sakihae tamae (8 times)

Power: The ability to transfer consciousness to inanimate objects, the empowerment of talismans. Dream magic and emotional transference. Astral projection. Healing and the transmutation of sunlight for alchemical purposes.

Age of the Gods (Nihon Shoki): **"After this Toyo-tama-hime fulfilled her promise, and, bringing with her-her younger sister, Tama-yori-hime, bravely confronted the winds and waves, and came to the sea-shore. When the time of her delivery was at hand, she besought Hiko-hoho-demi no Mikoto, saying: "When thy handmaiden is in travail, I pray thee do not look upon her." However, the Heavenly Grandchild could not restrain himself, but went secretly and peeped in. Now Toyo-tama-hime was just in childbirth, and had changed into a dragon. She was greatly ashamed, and said: "Hadst thou not disgraced me, I would have made the sea and land communicate with each other, and forever prevented them from being sundered. But now that thou hast disgraced me, wherewithal shall friendly feelings be knit together?" So she wrapped the infant inrushes, and abandoned it on the sea-shore. Then she barred the sea-path, and passed away. Accordingly the child was called Hiko-nagisa-take-u-gaya-fuki-ahezu no Mikoto... After this, when Toyo-tama-hime heard what a fine boy her child was, her heart was greatly moved with affection' and she wished to come back and bring him up herself. But she could not rightly do so, and therefore she sent her younger sister Tama-yori-hime to nurture him. Now when Toyotama-hime sent Tama-yori-hime,"**

Shortly after Hokihohodemi-no-Mikoto returned to land to settle things with his brother, his wife, Toyotama-hime-no-Mikoto, informed him that she was pregnant. Her pregnancy represents the beginning and nurturance of what is known as the spiritual embryo.

During the birth of Hikohohodemi-no-Mikoto's son, Toyotama-hime-no-Mikoto to her husband not to look in on her giving birth. Hikohohodemi-no-Mikoto, despite the word of his wife, looked in on her giving birth. In some accounts, she is said to have appeared as her true self, a black dragon, while giving birth. Ultimately, Toyotama-hime-no-Mikoto abandoned the child, instructing her sister, Tamayori-hime-no-Mikoto, to care for the newborn baby.

Tamayori-hime-no-Mikoto is the power of the subtle body. When the power of the subtle body is strengthened, the spiritual embryo grows. The fusion of the subtle body and the spiritual embryo causes the two to unite. In the Nihon Shoki, we are told:

"Now, when the child Hiko-nagisa-take-u-gaya-fuki-abezu no Mikoto grew up, he took his aunt Tama-yori-hime as his consort, and had by her in all four male children."

Tamayori-hime-no-Mikoto eventually wedded her nephew, a symbol of the alchemical marriage. Afterwards they had four children. The marriage represents the spirit and the four children, the four souls of the spirit. This story of Tamayori-hime-no-Mikoto represents what is known as Ichirei Shikon. Under the topic Mitama, Wikipedia reports:

"The most developed is the ichirei shikon (一霊四魂?), a Shinto theory according to which the spirit (霊魂, reikon?) of both kami and human beings consists of one spirit and four souls.[5] The four souls are the ara-mitama (荒御霊・荒御魂, rude soul?), the nigi-mitama (和御霊・和御魂, harmonious soul?), the saki-mitama (幸御魂, happy soul?) and the kushi-mitama (奇御霊・奇御魂, wondrous soul?). According to the theory, each of the souls making up the spirit has a character and a function of its own; they all exist at the same time, complementing each other."

The first letter in the Vasuh Power is P (16), or Zhee-Phe. This shows a direct reflection and purpose in the marriage of Izanagi-no-Mikoto and Izanami-no-Mikoto as compared with Tamayori-hime-no-Mikoto and Hiko-nagisatakeugayafukiabezu no Mikoto. In a similar manner to how Izanagi-no-Mikoto and Izanami-no-Mikoto, giving birth to the Sun Goddess, Amaterasu Ohmikami, the alchemical marriage of Tamayori-hime-no-Mikoto and Hiko-nagisatakeugayafukiabezu no Mikoto gives birth to an immortal spirit with four souls, or the sun and four seasons.

The next letter in the Vasuh power Phe is H (8), or Lewhu. Since Lewhu follows Zhee-Phe, we can determine that it is our initiation into the cosmic waters. Tamayori-hime-no-Mikoto represents the completion in a three-part initiatory process in the realms of the cosmic water. Up to the initiation point we have the sum of the Three Pure Ones:

P (16)-Zhee-Phe + H (8) Lewhu = 24 (PH)

Zhee = z (26) + h (8) + e (5) + e (5) = 44 = 4 + 4 = 8. The final sum of Zhee is 8.
Aum = a (1) + u (21) + m (13) = 35 = 3 + 5 = 8. The final sum of Aum is 8.
Tuu = t (20) + u (21) + u (21) = 62 = 6 + 2 = 8. The final sum of Tuu is 8.

8 + 8 + 8 = 24. 2 + 4 = 6. Six is Phe in the Vasuh language. We see that in the first two letters of Phe, P + H, an initiatory process, but one that also balances that of the starry realms as P (16) + H (8) equals 24, which is equivalent to the heavenly powers. We can say that the upper three Vasuh letters represent the realm of light and of fire. The next three Vasuh letters represent the Water and the deep. Interestingly, the Birth of the Crow, derive from the realm of Oho-Watatsumi-no-Mikoto. This information is confirmed in the Yi Jing Apocrypha of Genghis Khan.

Our final letter in the Vasuh power Phe is E (5). E is Bnhu in the Vasuh language. Five represents the one spirit and its four souls, or ichirei shikon. This is evident in the letter Bnhu as the Dragon Palace, Ryugujo, is described as such:

"**The inhabitants of the palace were Ryūjin's families and servants, who were <u>denizens</u> of the sea. In some legends, on** *each of the four sides of the palace it is a different <u>season</u>*,"

In the same manner that the initiate gains awareness of the one spirit and its four souls, it was also so for Ryugujo, the Dragon Palace, as it is surrounded by the four seasons. It is therefore the Sun behind the Sun, or the "spirit that gives the Sun its power." This is described for us in the Ivory Tablets of the Crow:

"**These operations must be sung in the light of the Goddess of the Sun. The Sun is a keeper of the records of men and sees all that occurs. And these words must be committed to the memory of thy heart, but can be recited before, for Shamuzi is the spirit that gives the Sun its power.**"

Tamayori-hime-no-Mikoto is of the race of the Shamuzi. In the same way that Tamayori-hime-no-Mikoto took care of the infant, the spiritual embryo, who she later married, this same process of one spirit and its four souls occur in the preliminary work of The Crow. In this case, the Soul of Fire prayer acts as the spirit and the Shamuzi the four souls of the spirit, as the Shamuzi has four distinct characteristics. Later in the text we read concerning the Baptism of the Ancient One, that the Bride of Nyarzir has four faces, another reference to the advancement of the Shamuzi.

In the Ivory Tablets of the Crow, we read about four distinct features of the Shamuzi. In the following passage we have inserted the names of the "four souls" next to their corresponding aspect found in the Shamuzi:

"**Now the lower part of the Shamuzi is like a horse (*nigi-mitama*) and the upper part is that of a beautiful woman with long golden hair (*saki-mitama*). Its eyes are like those of a cat (*kushi-mitama*) and in its teeth are the fangs of a bat (*ara-mitama*). However, its spirit is pure as a small child (*Soul of Fire*) for innocence is a valuable treasure that has long since been forgotten.**"

Usually, the Initiate will construct their altar by performing the Opening of the Sea ceremony prior to the Soul of Fire prayer. After the Soul of Fire prayer they are to call the Shamuzi. This is the science of the spiritual embryo. The Opening of the Sea represents the "water" that the embryo is contained in. Then, the Soul of Fire, symbolic of the actual embryo itself. This is followed by the call of the Shamuzi.

"**Now, when the child Hiko-nagisa-take-u-gaya-fuki-abezu no Mikoto grew up, he took his aunt Tama-yori-hime as his consort, and had by her in all four male children.**"

Nzu Mudra

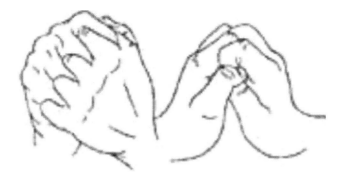

Vasuh Letter: ਪ੍ਰ

Mantra: Ame-no-Uzume-no-Mikoto, Saruta-hiko-no-Oho-kami mamori tamae sakihae tamae (6 times)

Power: Protection and astral martial arts. Thought transference. Can invoke arousal in others at a distance, or in close proximity, even to the point of orgasm. The ability to attack through dreams.

Age of the Gods (Nihon Shoki): "So Ame no Uzume forthwith bared breasts and pushing down the hand of her garment below her navel, confronted him with a mocking laugh. Then the God of the cross-ways asked her, saying: - 'Ame no Uzume! What meanest thou by this behavior?' She answered and said: - 'I venture to ask who art thou that dost remain in the road by which the child of Amaterasu no Oho-kami is to make progress?' The God of the cross-ways answered and said: - 'I have heard that the child of Amaterasu no Oho-kami is now about to descend, and therefore I have come respectfully to meet and attend upon him. My name is Saruta-hiko no Oho-kami.'

After the Initiate has journeyed from the stellar reason and into the ocean depths, where the Ancient Ones reside, this energy is then brought down to Earth. Saruta-hiko-no-Oho-Kami is of the race of the Tengu, though this information is not taught publicly. In the online *Encyclopedia of Shinto*, we read:

"**Sarutahiko was described as having a fantastic appearance, with a nose seven spans long, a height of over seven feet, and with eyes that glowed red like a mirror.**"

We get a bit more clarity into the meaning of Saruta-hiko-no-Oho-kami from the *Encyclopedia Mythica*. Under the topic, Sarutahiko Ohkami, written by Lisa Tonecek, we read:

"**The Japanese god of crossroads, pathways, and surmounting obstacles. He stands seven fathoms tall, with a massive beard and a jeweled spear. Holy light shines from his eyes, mouth, and posterior. Sarutahiko is the chief of the earthly kami and the husband of Ama-no-Uzume no Mikoto, the goddess of mirth, dancing, wifery, and health. He guards the bridge that links the heavens and the earth.**

When <u>Ninigi no Mikoto</u>, the August Grandson of <u>Amaterasu Ohmikami</u>, was preparing to descend to the earth and take possession of it, his scouts found that one earthly god remained rebellious and would not submit to Ninigi's rule. This was Sarutahiko, and as he guarded the Bridge of Heaven, Ninigi could not descend until the giant god swore fealty to him…. Having gotten his attention, Ama-no-Uzume insisted that he swear fealty to Ninigi and to Amaterasu, his grandmother. So impressed was Sarutahiko by the goddess' boldness that he immediately obeyed the command and at the same time asked her to be his wife."

Here we can see that Saruta-hiko-no-Oho-kami not only played an important role in the Shinto mysteries and the establishment of the heavenly jurisdiction on Earth, but also his relationship to the Tengu. He is described in the Encyclopedia of Shinto, as having "a nose seven spans long, a height of over seven feet." *The Mythical Creatures Bible*, by Brenda Rosen, states the following on page 373:

"In myth, the king of the *Tengu* is Sojobo, an ancient Yamabushi with long white hair and a long *nose*."

Saruta-hiko-no-Oho-kami is commonly translated as "monkey man." Some consider him an ancestor of the Tengu. One interesting thing about Saruta-hiko-no-Oho-kami, which is described in the Nihon Shoki:

"There is one God who dwells at the eight cross-roads of Heaven, the length of whose nose is seven hands, the length of whose back is more than seven fathoms."

Based on this passage, Saruta-hiko-no-Oho-kami is also a force that can be used as an aid, like Amaterasu Ohkami, in the work of "the eight cross-roads of Heaven," the Bagua of the Yi Jing. *The Tengu: Protectors of the Shinto Mysteries and Founders of the Art of Ninzuwu*, is the tile of an article appearing on the Art of Ninzuwu blog page. In the article, we read the following:

"Yatagarasu the Crow-God himself is symbolic specifically of guidance. This great crow was sent from heaven as a guide for <u>Emperor Jimmu</u> on his initial journey from the region which would become <u>Kumano</u> to what would become <u>Yamato</u>."

Yatagarasu was used by Amaterasu-Ohmikami to guide Emperor Jimmu. What is interesting is that the Yatagarsu means "eight-hand-crow." In the meaning of Yatagarasu, we do find that the "Crow-God" was of the race of the Tengu. In Ninzuwu-Shinto metaphysics the term "eight-hand-crow" is symbolic of "eight crossroads of heaven," often noted by another guide, who escorted Amaterasu-Ohmikami's grandson Ninigi, <u>Sarutahiko-Ohkami</u>."

Here we see not only a connection, but progression in understanding how Saruta-hiko-no-Oho-kami relates to the Nzu Mudra. The Vasuh power Phe is symbolic of Tamayori-hime-no-Mikoto. It was discussed that she nursed the "spiritual embryo." As the embryo grows it is nurtured by "divine knowledge" and matures to establish its own place in the workings of the divine world. This process occurs as the Initiate moves from a basic understanding of the Ivory Tablets of the Crow to the deeper aspects of practicing the Art of Ninzuwu. Saruta-hiko-no-Oho-kami went out to meet the grandson of Amaterasu Ohkami, Ninigi, (symbolic of the Initiate), at the eight-cross roads of Heaven.

It is the process of bringing heavenly knowledge down to Earth that is the lesson here. Saruta-hiko-no-Oho-kami acted as the protector of the grandson of Amaterasu Ohkami. Nzu is a sign of protection. In the Ivory Tablets of the Crow, concerning Nzu, it states:

"Can be used as a protective shield, or to heal cuts and wounds."

Before Saruta-hiko-no-Oho-kami acted as protector of Ninigi, the grandson of Amaterasu Ohmikami, it was Ninigi who sent Ame-no-Uzume-no-Mikoto out to meet Saruta-hiko-no-Oho-kami to determine if he was an enemy or not. Ame-no-Uzume-no-Mikoto opened the way for Ninigi by appeasing Saruta-hiko-no-Oho-kami through her flirtatious demeanor. She was honored with the title, which became a lineage, known as Sarume-no-Kimi, or monkey women. W. G. Aston, English translator of the Nihon Shoki, writes:

"The Sarume were primarily women who performed comic dances (saru-mahi or monkey-dances) in honour of the Gods. They are mentioned along with the Nakatomi and Imbe as taking part in the festival of first-fruits and other Shinto ceremonies. These dances were the origin of the Kagura and No performances. Another function of the Sarume is that indicated in the part taken by Uzume no Mikoto when the Gods enticed the Sun-Goddess out of her rock-cave. She is there said to have been divinely inspired. This divine inspiration has always been common in Japan. The inspired person Cadis into a trance, or hypnotic stale, in which he or she speaks in the character of some God. Such persons are now known as Miko, defined by Hepburn as 'a woman who, dancing in a Miya, pretends to hold communication with the Gods and the spirits of the dead,' in short a medium."

Ame-no-Uzume-no-Mikoto was an aid, not only to Ninigi's mission of establishing Heaven on Earth, but in luring Amaterasu Ohkami out of the rock-cave. Wikipedia reports:

"Amaterasu's brother, the storm god <u>Susano'o</u>, had vandalized her rice fields, threw a flayed horse at her loom, and brutally killed one of her maidens due to a quarrel between them. In turn, Amaterasu became furious with him and retreated into the Heavenly Rock Cave, <u>Amano-Iwato</u>. The world, without the illumination of the sun, became dark and the gods could not lure Amaterasu out of her hiding place.

The clever Uzume overturned a tub near the cave entrance and began a dance on it, tearing off her clothing in front of the other deities. They considered this so comical that they laughed heartily at the sight. This dance is said to have founded the Japanese ritual dance, <u>Kagura</u>.

Amaterasu heard them, and peered out to see what all the fuss was about. When she opened the cave, she saw her glorious reflection in a mirror which Uzume had placed on a tree, and slowly emerged from her hiding spot."

Ame-no-Uzume-no-Mikoto represents an advanced stage of Tamayori-hime-no-Mikoto in relation to the spiritual embryo. Whereas, Tamayori-hime-no-Mikoto represents the Shamuzi, Ame-no-Uzume-no-Mikoto represents the Shamuzi's transformation into the Ayaqox. The Ivory Tablets of the Crow describes the Ayaqox in the "eight cross-roads of Heaven:

"She left this world and found her place in the Realm of Eternal Lust. Her dwelling place is full of clouds and flashes of lightening. It is said that even the ground She walks upon will appear as cloud of heaven."

She imparts a certain initiation described in the Ivory Tablets of the Crow as the Stone Bowl of Eternity. The Stone Bowl of Eternity represents the transmutation of the sexual energy. This is a necessary act in the work of immortality. Taoist author, His Lai wrote in the following in his work entitled; *White Tigress*:

"The physical goal of the White Tigress is to first recreate the sexual responses in her body that were initially developed during adolescence, which would aid the development of her physical restoration. Since the majority of our first libidinal developments occur within oral activities (production of saliva, suckling breast milk, developing the oratory functions, and forming of teeth), the White Tigress equally finds the development of youthfulness and immortality within the activities of oral functions……It is the practice of Absorbing the Dragon's Breath that leads to the spiritual achievement of Illumination—the experience of seeing numerous, small, lantern-like lights swaying gently inside the head. The White Tigress needs *to experience this illumination nine separate times* in order to produce sufficient energy to create her Spiritual Fetus, or in more practical terms to realize her spiritual potential.

Creating this spiritual fetus is like undergoing the metamorphosis from mortality to immortality, or like going from blindness to sight. In every sense it is like a spiritual pregnancy whereupon she gives birth to the spiritual fetus within herself, much like a caterpillar shedding its cocoon and emerging as a butterfly."

Ame-no-Uzume-no-Mikoto appears in Babylonian mythology as the goddess Ishtar. She precedes Saruta-hiko-no-Oho-kami in the mantra, for she is a skilled warrior herself and knows that the invisible force of sexual energy is the greatest weapon, even in physical defense.

The first letter in the Vasuh power Nzu is N (14), or Zhee-Hmu. Here we see on the path of descent the finding of a kingdom. This represents Ame-no-Uzume-no-Mikoto being sent by Ninigi to Saruta-hiko-no-Oho-kami. Zhee-Hmu equals Bnhu, or $1 + 4 = 5$. This represents the establishment of a rite, depicted in the said mythology concerning Ninigi, but also similar to Oho-Watatsumi-no-Mikoto's way.

The next letter in the Vasuh power Nzu is Z (26), or Aum-Phe. Ame-no-Uzume-no-Mikoto appears again in this equation, as her name means "dawn." Aum is the Sun Goddess Amaterasu Ohkami. Phe is nurturing the spiritual embryo through a solar means, as $2 + 6 = 8$, Lewhu. This is followed by the Vasuh power U (21), or Aum-Zhee. $2 + 1 = 3$, or Tuu. The Tengu are ruled by Tsukiyomi-no-Mikoto. The union of Ame-no-Uzume-no-Mikoto and Saruta-hime-no-Oho-kami represents the union of solar and lunar forces within the Initiate. Among the ancient Ninzuwu, what many scholars call the Naacals and the Nagas, earth is where the unification of these forces can be experienced.

Lewhu Mudra

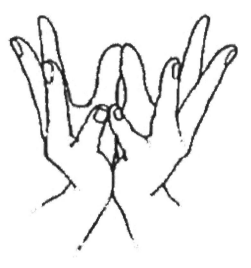

Vasuh Letter:

Mantra: Ama-tsu-hiko-hiko-ho-Ninigi-no-Mikoto mamori tamae sakihae tamae (6 times)

Power: The cultivation of good luck in one's personal affairs and the ability to bestow good luck upon others.

Age of the Gods (Nihon Shoki): "**The two Gods thereupon ascended to Heaven and reported the result of their mission, saying:—'All the Central Land of Reed-Plains is now completely tranquillized.' Now Ama-terasu no Oho-kami gave command, saying: — 'If that be so, I will send down my child.' She was about to do so, when in the meantime, an August Grandchild was born, whose name was called Ama-tsu-hiko-hiko-ho-no-ninigi no Mikoto. Her son represented to her that he wished the August Grandchild to be sent down in his stead. Therefore Ama-terasu no Oho-kami gave to Ama-tsu-hiko-hiko-ho no ninigi no Mikoto the three treasures, viz. the curved jewel of Yasaka gem, the eight-hand mirror, and the sword Kusanagi, and joined to him as his attendants Ame no Koyane no Mikoto, the first ancestor of the Naka-tomi, Futo-dama no Mikoto, the first ancestor of the Imbe, Ame no Uzume no Mikoto, the first ancestor of the Sarume,' Ishi-kori-dome no Mikoto, the first ancestor of the mirror-makers, and Tamaya no Mikoto, the first ancestor of the jewel-makers, in all Gods of five Be. Then she commanded her August Grandchild, saying: — 'This Reed-plain-1500-autumns-fair-rice-ear Land is the region which my descendants shall be lords of. Do thou, my August Grandchild, proceed thither and govern it. Go! And may prosperity attend thy dynasty, and may it, like Heaven and Earth, endure forever."**

Ama-tsu-hiko-hiko-ho-ninigi-no-Mikoto is popularly known as Ninigi-no-Mikoto. Ninigi-no-Mikoto was sent by Amaterasu Ohkami to the central land of the reed plains, what would later become known as Japan. Amaterasu Ohkami also gave Ninigi-no-Mikoto three signs of his charge: a jewel (symbolizing benevolence), a mirror (purity), and Kusanagi, the "grass-mowing" sword (courage). The jewel, the mirror, and the sword are still the Japanese Imperial symbols. There is much symbolism and meaning behind the legacy of Ninigi-no-Mikoto that we will now discuss.

The letter of the Vasuh power Lewhu is L (12), or Zhee-Aum. In this case, Zhee-Aum is a solar aspect of what is next to follow. We can determine this as the numbers are running in a coherent manner, increasing instead of decreasing as they are read. This is symbolic of the sunrise, or the rising sun. The sun appears to increase in light while traveling through the sky. We are reminded of Ninigi's journey in this regard being sent by his ancestor Amaterasu Ohkami into the world to establish order. In a similar manner the Initiate is able to discern his purpose in life and others in his experience, for the Initiate descended from the Aum to reach the initiation of Lewhu. The legend of Ninigi-no-Mikoto is a personified account of the schools and universities established by the Naacals, or Nagas, when the Empire of Mu flourished.

The next letter that appears in the Vasuh power is E (5), or Bnhu. We can see that while the mythological account of Ninigi-no-Mikoto states that the Imperial symbols, the jewel (symbolizing benevolence), a mirror (purity), and Kusanagi, the "grass-mowing" sword (courage), were given to him by Amaterasu Ohkami, these things are acquired during one's initiation. We can that in the letter Bnhu (E) that the initiate is trying to establish a kingdom too. Ninigi-no-Mikoto is Nyarlathotep of Lovecraftian fiction. He is the personification of a priesthood whose legacy can be found in times of remote antiquity.

We come now to the letter W (23), or Aum-Tuu. Ninigi-no-Mikoto represents the Initiate who has heard the call for the work of the greater good, and due to such, has obtained the initiation of the primordial realm, Zhee-Aum (L), the watery depths, Bnhu (E), and the powers of the sun and moon, Aum-Tuu, W (23). In this we find the three treasures of Amaterasu Ohkami. L (12), Zhee-Aum, the primordial power, is found in the "mirror." E (5), Bnhu, the inner alchemy of benevolence, is found in the jewel. W (23), Aum-Tuu, the power of the sun and moon, is found in the "grass-mowing" sword, Kusanagi, which was originally known as Ame-no-Murakumo-no-Tsurugi, "Sword of the Gathering Clouds of Heaven."

The next letter of the Vasuh power Lewhu is H (8), Lewhu. Lewhu relates not only to the "divine energies of the stars," but illustrates that the Vasuh language is primordial. The term Vasuh has the same value as Enochian.

Lewhu in English Gematria Equals: **414** (l e w h u / 72 30 138 48 126)

Lewhu in Simple Gematria Equals: **69** (l e w h u / 12 5 23 8 21)

Enochian in English Gematria Equals: **414** (e n o c h i a n / 30 84 90 18 48 54 6 84)

Enochian in Simple Gematria Equals: **69** (e n o c h i a n / 5 14 15 3 8 9 1 14)

The next and last letter in this Vasuh power is U (21), or Aum-Zhee. Since Aum-Zhee follows the starry initiatory properties of H, or Lewhu, Aum-Zhee's appearance at the end of Lewhu would represent and aspect of the dark moon, a time when one can focus on the stars. Aum-Zhee, in this case, is the ability to confer initiation, to rule a kingdom. Lewhu is the only Vasuh power with 5 letters, "one spirit, and four souls."

Shki Mudra

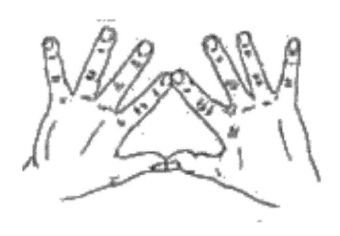

Vasuh Letter: 𝔐

Mantra: Shiho-tsutsu-no-oji-no-Mikoto mamori tamae sakihae tamae (6 times)

Power: The ability to eradicate past karma for oneself and those of others. Can acquire money and other treasures by mysterious means. Ancestor worship through telepathic communication. An understanding of deep and profound things. The ability to cure impotency by touch or at a distance. He is the ruler of the shikigami. Shikigami are the Shamuzi.

Age of the Gods (Nihon Shoki): **"The younger brother remained by the sea-shore grieving and making moan, when he met with Shiho-tsutsu no Oji, who inquired of him, saying:- 'Why dost thou grieve in this way?' Ho no ori no Mikoto answered and said, etc., etc...The old man said: 'Grieve no longer. I will devise a plan."**

Shiho-tsutsu-no-Oji-no-Mikoto is referred to in various accounts as the Ancient One of the Sea and Sea-Salt Elder. He is the Lord of the Earth and one of the oldest deities known to modern man. There is not must written about him. However, the ancient accounts that feature him, all seem to illustrate his hospitable manner. Shiho-tsutsu-no-Mikoto is also known as Kotokatsu kunikatsunagasa no Mikoto. In the Encyclopedia of Shinto, we read:

"A local kami who greeted the heavenly grandchild Ninigi upon his arrival at Kasasa of Ata no Nagaya (in Kagoshima Prefecture) after his descent from heaven (tenson kōrin). Nihongi states that the kami made a free-will offering of the land to Ninigi. According to a variant "alternate writing" also provided by Nihongi, the kami is identified with Shiotsuchi no oji ("old man of the sea"), an offspring of Izanagi. Shiotsuchi no oji is described elsewhere as guiding Hohodemi to the Palace of the Sea, and telling Emperor Jinmu about the "fair land to the east," with the result that he is viewed as a tutelary kami of the sea."

Shiho-tsutsu-no-oji-no-Mikoto is described in the Encyclopedia of Shinto as an offspring of Izanagi-no-Mikoto. If we remember, earlier in our discussion, we spoke about the belief of "one spirit, four souls" applying to both kami and humans. In this case, Izanagi-no-Mikoto, the yang principle, also has one spirit and four souls. These are the realms of air, fire, water, and earth. In the early records of the Nihon Shoki the sentient beings of all these elements were able to interact and communicate with each other as they do today. Human beings, however, are not attuned to this process of communication for the most part. The beginning of the Nihon Shoki gives a detailed report of how the "heavenly deities" interacted with the "earthly deities." Based on such, we can say the same for Izanami-no-Mikoto, the yin principle. The intercourse of the yin and yang principles amounts to eight souls, giving origin to the Yi Jing. The teaching of "one spirit, four souls" explains how a person can appear in the dreams of others vividly, but may not recall the experience themselves. Shiho-tsutsu-no-oji-no-Mikoto represents the personified earth soul of both Izanagi-no-Mikoto and Izanami-no-Mikoto's union. Shiho-tsutsu-no-oji-no-Mikoto is the race of the Naacals, Nagas, but proper in their own language of Mu, the Ninzuwu.

Shiho-tsutsu-no-oji-no-Mikoto always appears as an elderly man or woman. *Old Age in Pre-Nara and Nara Periods* by Susanne Formanek, mentions the following:

"Looking at the earliest written monuments of Japanese culture, old people are indeed first mentioned as holding the status of gods, or rather, gods appear in the shape of old people..... This similarity or closeness of the aged with the souls of the dead is also suggested by the word *kamusabu* **as used in the** *Manyôshû*. **Meaning literally „to behave, act like a god", this word is used to describe the transformation of the souls of the dead into gods as well as the ageing of things and of persons. The pertaining to or being connected with the other world which thus characterized the** *okina* **is also exemplified by the already mentioned Shiho-tsutsu-no-oji. In the** *Nihon shoki* **variants of the Yama-no-sachi legend he is the one helping Yama-no-sachi to reach the Palace of the Sea God, which can be interpreted to be related to that other world beyond the sea where the souls of the dead went to. The whole episode seems to be a mythical relation of a kind of initiation rite in which the initiand is made to die a symbolic death to come back to life provided with the knowledge of the other world and may hint at the fact that in the remote past of Japan's history old men played the part of the initiator in initiation rites of this kind."**

In the Ivory Tablets of the Crow, the Ninzuwu are described as follows:

"The Ninzuwu may visit the person of these operations in physical form, usually as one ripe in years."

Shiho-tsutsu-no-oji-no-Mikoto is not a force that is invoked to obtain things without any effort. He works in assisting those who are truly working hard. In the case of Hohodemi, Shiho-tsutsu-no-oji-no-Mikoto only appeared to him after he was grieving by the ocean. He came out to Ninigi-no-Mikoto after he was on his journey and gave him a free will offering of land. Life is about hard work. We are here to work. Work is a blessing from the gods.

The first letter in the Vasuh power Shiki is S (19), or Zhee-Shki. Shiho-tsutsu-no-oji-no-Mikoto is the man of completion, like Zhee-Shki, it encompasses the whole. In life there is said to be three classes of people, the rich, the middle-class, and the poor. This is patterned after life itself, where we see the elderly (rich), adult (middle-class), and the poor (children). Zhee-Shki is our path.
The next letter in the Vasuh power Shki is H (8), or Lewhu. Once again we see an initiation. While there are "initiations" we may experience, some voluntarily, and others by chance in life, initiation is an eternal process. Initiation is a state of being. It is a state of being known as immortality. Regardless of our status in life, there is still more work to do. In order for us to reach other levels, we must participate in some form of initiation, even if it means changing one's habits. Initiation is how we travel from one experience to the next. This is how we determine if someone is sleeping or in control of their life.

A sleeping person is just riding the wave of life. They let life carry them from one experience to the next. Those who are in control of their lives, imagines their experiences, he or she has, before entering them. We will discuss this in more detail in the *Walking with the Sun* exercise. The eternal process of initiation is discussed symbolically in the Ivory Tablets of the Crow, where we read:

"Seek only initiation...For initiation is the only law that is just unto man"

The next letter in the Vasuh power Shki is K (11), or Zhee-Zhee. It is by our initiation that we are able to come to an understanding of the process of life, the book of Changes. It's not about life. It's about awareness and awareness will use life's changes for the cultivation of itself.

The spirituality of Mu was very simple indeed, for it is the study of awareness in life, and how such is cultivated. It is by the Art of Ninzuwu that we come to know of this awareness. This Art is practiced today by making use of the metaphysical meanings of both the Shinto and the Yi Jing. This is illustrated in the advanced understanding of the Soul of Fire:

Zhee = 44 = 4 + 4 = 8
Aum = 35 = 3 + 5 = 8
Tuu = 62 = 6 + 2 = 8

8 x 3 = 24, 2 + 4 = 6

The equation above illustrates the sum of the "heavenly aspect" of the Soul of Fire. Its sum is six, or Phe. Phe is relative to Tamayori-hime-no-Mikoto, or feeding the spiritual embryo. Yet, it also relates to the goddess Amaterasu Ohkami as we find in the Nihon Shoki:

"The resplendent lustre of this child shone throughout all the six quarters."

The six quarters are North, South, East, West, both Above and Below. North, South, East, and West, equals, four directions above, and four directions below. 4 + 4 = 8. Eight is the foundation of the Yi Jing, the Bagua. 8 x 8 = 64.

Here we see that each Vasuh letter of "upper heaven" is equal to eight, which means that it is perfect unto itself, but collectively work as the hexagram of heaven. Now let us look at the "middle heavens."

Hmu = 42 = 4 + 2 = 6
Bnhu = 45 = 4 + 5 = 9
Phe =   29 = 2 + 9 = 11

6 + 9 + 11 = 26, 2 + 6 = 8

The sum of the "middle heavens" is eight, Lewhu. It relates to the waters of initiation, the cosmic influence of change itself. The "middle heavens" is ruled by Oho-Watatsumi-no-Mikoto, the Dragon King. Here we see a confirmation of an observation, cited earlier, by Susanne Formanek:

"The pertaining to or being connected with the other world which thus characterized the *okina* is also exemplified by the already mentioned Shiho-tsutsu-no-oji. In the *Nihon shoki* variants of the Yama-no-sachi legend he is the one helping Yama-no-sachi to reach the Palace of the Sea God, which

can be interpreted to be related to that other world beyond the sea where the souls of the dead went to. The whole episode seems to be a mythical relation of a kind of initiation rite in which the initiand is made to die a symbolic death to come back to life provided with the knowledge of the other world and may hint at the fact that in the remote past of Japan's history old men played the part of the initiator in initiation rites of this kind."

The "middle heavens" is necessary for our evolution, but is not necessary for life itself. It is a hidden force, as its sum is eight. Individually, however, these powers are somewhat radical, which can be evidenced by their individual sum. The Book of Nine Dreams, appearing in the Ivory Tablets of the Crow, is the Book of the Dragon King. Now let us take a look at the "lower heavens," or earth.

Nzu = 61 = 6 + 1 = 7
Lewhu = 69 = 6 + 9 = 15
Shki = 47 = 4 + 7 = 11

7 + 15 + 11 = 33, 3 + 3 = 6

The sum of the Earth is six, or Phe. Earth is a direct reflection of the "upper heavens." Communication, mediumship between the lower and upper heavens can be had by those who hare of the realm of the "middle heavens," which stands in between the upper and lower regions.

Vasuh is the language of light. Light carries thought. In the Ivory Tablets of the Crow, we are told that the Vasuh letters relate the "energies of the Great Bear constellation." This would include the stars of the Big Dipper, the North Star, and several other stars. Of course, as it has been referred to in several writings online, the Vasuh letters would refer to the North Star and the energies of the Big Dipper. In the Introduction of the Ivory Tablets of the Crow, it states:

"The Ivory Tablets describe what seems to be an initiatory journey into what is known today as pure consciousness. Obtainment of this divine state required that one hold intercourse with several "dark stars," or what the mystics of Nyarzir called "crows."

These dark stars are discussed in the writings of Dr. Jerry A. Johnson:

"The ancient Daoists also believed in the existence of certain "anti-stars," stars that could not be seen with the eyes but existed as counterparts to the visible stars. They therefore positioned the existence of these invisible Dipper stars around the location of the visible stars...According to ancient Daoist texts, the nine stars of the Big Dipper constellations are doubled in number by virtue of their association with a group of nine dark stars, which cast a "black light," or "light that does not shine." This is a type of sacred darkness floating around the North Pole. The black light is also associated with the "floating darkness" where nothing external or internal can be seen...These nine dark stars are actually the stars of the celestial Hun and Po, or Ling Ming (Magical Light) wherein female deities known as the "Nine Empresses of the Great Yin" dwell. The Nine Empresses of the Great Yin are associated with the condition of *Wu Wei*, in which the forces of nature are gathered and hidden. They were also believed to assist the Daoist adept in the art of advanced physical, energetic, and spiritual transformation."

If we add up the values of each Vasuh letter, we find something interesting:

Zhee = 44
Aum = 35

Tuu = 62

The Upper Heavens is equal to: 44 + 35 + 62 = 141. The Upper Heavens is 141.

Hmu = 42
Bnhu = 45
Phe = 29

The Middle Heavens is equal to 42 + 45 + 29 = 116

Nzu = 61
Lewhu = 69
Shki = 47

The Lower Heavens is equal to 61 + 69 + 47 = 177

The Soul of Fire equals 141 + 116 + 177 = 434 The Soul of Fire = 434. Here we see an "actual fact" in Ninzuwu metaphysics. Actual facts are subject to change, especially when said to describe celestial events. However, the significance of the number 434 is seen in a Wikipedia article discussing the North Star, entitled, Polaris:

"Many recent papers calculate the distance to Polaris at about 434 light-years (133 parsecs). Some suggest it may be 30% closer which, if correct, is especially notable because Polaris is the closest Cepheid variable to Earth, so its physical parameters are of critical importance to the whole astronomical distance scale."

It was long held that Polaris is 434 light-years away from Earth. Of course, this distance is subject to change in the course of time. Yet, this is quite interesting, as there is a correspondence between the number 434 and the Big Dipper, even in the field of astronomy. Ultimately, 434 equals Aum, 4 + 3 + 4 = 11, 1 +1 = 2.

Aum is the realm of Amaterasu Ohkami. Her sacred animal is the crow, based on the Yatagarasu. Her number is 9. In simple gematria the sum of Amaterasu is 99. Aum is said to carry the powers of Zhee to any distant location. The Art of Ninzuwu is the cultivation of the Zhee, for purposes that best fulfill the aims of the Divine World.

The Empowerment of Takama no Hara

During the initiation, as given in the Ivory Tablets of the Crow, the candidate passes through the "nine dreams" and unknowingly obtains use of the "tide jewels." The Bride of Nyarzir is Amaterasu Ohkami. She is described as the bride with four faces, representing the "sun and four seasons," or the "sun and the four cardinal points of the zodiac." We discussed Ichirei Shikon earlier, one spirit, four souls. This would also apply to Amaterasu as the one spirit, and the four souls, as the four seasons, the four cardinal points of the zodiac. She is described in the Ivory Tablets of the Crow, as a 'woman wearing a white dress with no legs.' This represents a heavenly force, one that doesn't walk on the ground, or without legs.

Amaterasu Ohkami is the personification of the Art of Ninzuwu. She, like ourselves, has visited the watery depths of the Dragon King and gained the vital "initiation." After obtaining such, she rose up to the heavens to let her glory shine. According to the *Oxford Encyclopedia of Women in World History* by Bonnie G. Smith, we read the following little-known fact about Amaterasu Ohkami:

"The archaic society of Japan, according to Robert Ellwood, was horticultural and matrilineal, worshipped a *sea goddess* named *Amaterasu*, and used shaman priestesses as intermediaries."

After the Baptism of the Ancient One, the Initiate must learn how to rise up to the heavens. Similar to the initial Soul of Fire initiation, found in the early stages, and mentioned in the lessons on the Ivory Tablets of the Crow, the Initiate must invoke one mudra each day for nine days.

(Empowerment of the Mudra.)This means that the Initiate must take the first mudra, Zhee, and perform the Zhee Mudra, with its mantra, through each of the nine chakras and then back up to the crown. The Zhee mantra must be recited six times in each chakra, while holding the hands in the mudra position seen in the illustration. Once the Initiate has reached the ninth chakra, they should perform the cleansing breath and then do the Zhee Mudra, and its mantra of six times in each chakra in the ascending motion. One mudra, with its mantra, must be done each day through all nine chakras in a descending, then ascending pattern, finishing at the Zhee Chakra. PLEASE NOTE THAT THERE IS A PRELIMINARY STEP BEFORE ENGAGIING IN THE EMPOWERMENT OF THE NINE MUDRAS.

Step 1: Make a clear space and get into a comfortable position, facing North or East. Use the Cleansing Breathe to clear your mind.

Step 2: Clap three times. Then repeat "Jo-huta" three times.

Step 3: Perform the Soul of Fire Prayer, as taught in the Ivory Tablets of the Crow, three times.

Step 4: Pray giving thanks to the source of your awareness, Johuta. Give thanks for the use of your awareness. Give thanks to all the "invisible" forces, gods, and guides that have aided you on your spiritual path. Give thanks to the ancestors. Pray for those in need in other areas of the world. Pray for those in need and various situation in your homeland. Pray for the welfare of your family. Pray for friends and co-workers. Pray for one's own being.

Step 5: Clap you hand three times.

Step 6: Two bows, two claps, one bow.

Step 7: Perform the Prayer of Heaven (Amatsu Norito) 3 times:

Prayer of Heaven

Taka ama hari ni Kamu zumari masu Kamurogi Kamuromi no Mikoto moshite
Sumemi oya Kamu Izanagi no Ohkami Tsukushi no Himuka no Tachibana no
Odo no Awagigahara ni Misogi harae tamaishi Toki ne are mase-ru
Harae do no Ohkami tachi Moromoro no Maga goto Tsumi kegare o
Harae tamae Kiyome tamae to Maosu kotono Yoshi o
Amatsu kami Kunitsu kami Yao yorozu no Kami tachi tomo ni Kikoshi mese to
Kashi komi Kashi komi mo mao su

Step 8: Perform the Empowerment of the Mudra.

Step 9: Connect with the ruling Kami of the said mudra. Express your gratitude and thanks. Do not make any requests during the Empowerment initiation process. Just give thanks.

Step 10: Recite KAN NAGARA TAMACHI HAMASE (3 times)

Step 11: two bows, two claps, one bow. The rite has ended.

These empowerments can be very intense at times. Please follow the instructions careful and keep a pure intent. There may be times when you may lose count of the chant in a chakra or what have you. In cases such as these, just pick up where you left off. Recite the mantra for the said amount of repetitions and move on to the next chakra.

During the nine days of empowerment, it is good to drink extra water and avoid toxic substances. You may also find it beneficial to look at some of the sources for pronunciation purposes. The recitation of the Amatsu Norito is online.

Once you have completed the Nine Day Empowerment of Takama no Hara your initiation is complete. You must then learn how to use the Armor of Amaterasu Ohkami. Aum is the Vasuh letter associate with Amaterasu Ohkami. Interestingly, Amaterasu Ohkami is also "a race of watchers" that we call the Ninzuwu. The sum of Ninzuwu equals Aum. Ninzuwu equals 128, 1 + 2 + 8 = 11. 1 + 1 = Aum (2).

The Armor of Amaterasu Ohkami

After the Empowerment of Takama no Hara, the Initiate is prepared to wear the Armor of Amaterasu Ohkami. This is ritual is best to be performed daily. Over time, the Initiate will grow in understanding and wisdom. They will develop a renewed energy and sense of purpose as they communicate with the Divine World. Please Note: THIS IS NOT AN EXPERIMENTAL EXERCISE AND SHOULD NEVER BE PERFORMED AS AN EXPERIMENT. The Initiate should be serious about their practice, as having undergone the Baptism of the Ancient One. Daily exercise of the said rite should replace one's addiction to entertainment forms. PRACTICE DAILY WHEN POSSIBLE.

Once the initiate understands how to invoke the Armor of Amaterasu Ohkami, they can then employ the one of the nine powers for beneficent purpose. Putting on the Armor of Amaterasu Ohkami consists of the following steps:

Step 1: Make a clear space and get into a comfortable position, facing North or East. Use the Cleansing Breathe to clear your mind.

Step 2: Clap three times. Then repeat "Johuta" three times.

Step 3: Perform the Soul of Fire Prayer, as taught in the Ivory Tablets of the Crow, three times.

Step 4: Pray giving thanks to the source of your awareness, Johuta. Give thanks for the use of your awareness. Give thanks to all the "invisible" forces, gods, and guides that have aided you on your spiritual path. Give thanks to the ancestors. Pray for those in need in other areas of the world. Pray for those in need and various situations in your homeland. Pray for the welfare of your family. Pray for friends and co-workers. Pray for one's own being.

Step 5: Clap you hand three times.

Step 6: Two bows, two claps, one bow.

Step 7: Perform the Prayer of Heaven (Amatsu Norito) 3 times:

Prayer of Heaven

Taka ama hari ni Kamu zumari masu Kamurogi Kamuromi no Mikoto moshite
Sumemi oya Kamu Izanagi no Ohkami Tsukushi no Himuka no Tachibana no
Odo no Awagigahara ni Misogi harae tamaishi Toki ne are maser u
Harae do no Ohkami tachi Moromoro no Maga goto Tsumi kegare o
Harae tamae Kiyome tamae to Maosu kotono Yoshi o

The Armor of Amaterasu Ohkami

Amatsu kami Kunitsu kami Yao yorozu no Kami tachi tomo ni Kikoshi mese to
Kashi komi Kashi komi mo mao su

Step 8: Invoke each of the mudra and recite its mantra for its corresponding chakra. When the Initiate has descended from Zhee to Shki, perform the cleansing breathe. Afterwards, perform the ascending motion from Shki to Zhee.

The Armor of Amaterasu Ohkami

1. Vasuh Letter:

Mantra: Izanagi-no-Mikoto, Izanami-no-Mikoto mamori tamae sakihae tamae (6 times)

2. Vasuh Letter:

Mantra: A-ma-te-ra-su-O-ho-mi-ka-mi (6 times)

3. Vasuh Letter:

Mantra: Tsukiyomi-no-Mikoto mamori tamae sakihae tamae (6 times)

4. Vasuh Letter:

Mantra: Toyotama-hime-no-Mikoto mamori tamae sakihae tamae (8 times)

5. Vasuh Letter:

Mantra: Ryu-gu-jo, Oho-Watatsumi-no-Mikoto mamori tamae sakihae tamae (8 times)

6.  Vasuh Letter: ﻭ

Mantra: Tamayori-hime-no-Mikoto mamori tamae sakihae tamae (8 times)

7. Vasuh Letter: ५

Mantra: Ame-no-Uzume-no-Mikoto, Saruta-hiko-no-Oho-kami mamori tamae sakihae tamae (6 times)

8.  Vasuh Letter: ᾰᵗᵸ

Mantra: Ama-tsu-hiko-hiko-ho-ninigi-no-Mikoto mamori tamae sakihae tamae (6 times)

9. Vasuh Letter: ᛀ

Mantra: Shiho-tsutsu-no-oji-no-Mikoto mamori tamae sakihae tamae (6 times)

Step 9: Pray, giving thanks to the Kami. Pray for the ancestors. Pray concerning the conditions of the world. Pray for family and close relatives. Pray for co-workers, friends, and neighbors. Pray for one's own being in accordance with the divine will.

Step 10: (Optional) After these things have been performed, the initiate may invoke one of the Vasuh powers by holding its mudra and reciting the accompanying mantra through all nine chakras in a descending pattern, from Zhee to Shki, and then ascending from Shki to Zhee.

Conclusion: Recite KAN NAGARA TAMACHI HAMASE (3 times). This is followed by two bows, two claps, and one bow.

When the Initiate performs the "optional" step after putting on the Armor of Amaterasu Ohkami, they must close their eyes, still holding the mudra, and express a deep sincere thanks for the gift and opportunity of such, and that their working is in accord with the will of the Divine World. They are to then to proceed with a visualization of them exercising the power that is invoked to the finest detail possible, while pushing the breath into the imagination. The other realm will open in the mind. One must whisper while the visualization is taking place, all that they would like to occur. This whispering must be in a low voice and "serpent-like."

Walking With the Sun

Our lives are dependent on the breathing process. There is law in breath, for in our breath is our only obligation to the creator. There are several sections in this text that mention the "cleansing breath." The cleansing breath is a very simple, but effective method of cleansing our energy body. We should perform the cleansing breath every day after awakening from sleep.

We perform the cleansing breath by inhaling, for an eighth-count. Next, exhale by an eighth-count, pushing the air out of our bodies with a hissing noise. We perform this three times. This is the cleansing breath. It is very effective for ridding oneself of useless habits like smoking

Another important exercise that helps strengthen the mind of the Initiate is the Walking with the Sun exercise. If performed daily, one will see miraculous occur over time.

Step 1: Perform the cleansing breath.

Step 2: Two bows, two claps, one bow.

Step 3: Imagine a glowing white ball of light within the Aum chakra. Begin chanting "A-ma-te-ra-su-O-ho-mi-ka-mi." The chanting should continue throughout the whole exercise. Can be done in an undertone.

Step 4: Imagine that the light from the Aum chakra is the Sun shining during the day.

Step 5: Now imagine that you are looking into the face of the Sun on a clear day.

Step 6: Imagine how you would like to see your day begin and end. During this visualization, the Sun will move through the sky from sunrise to sunset. When the mind drifts away from the visualization, gain focus by imagining yourself looking into the face of the Sun on a clear day.

Step 7: After the visualization is complete, two bows, two claps, one bow.

The Walking with the Sun exercise is an excellent way to build focus and concentration. It is useful in fighting off negative thinking and depression. It also assists in the development of astral projection. It is a great way to begin our day. One should also keep a journal of the visualizations they employed during this exercise.

Creating a Shrine of Ninzuwu

Building a sacred place in one's home or experience is a vital part of our spiritual practice. In the Art of Ninzuwu creating a sacred space can be enjoyed regardless if we have a home or not. It is something that can even be enjoyed by a homeless person. In the Art of Ninzuwu, one's shrine is connected with practitioner's relationship to plants and trees. This information was touched upon briefly in this writing under the topic Hmu:

"Hikohohodemi-no-Mikoto is said to have stood at the foot of the cassia-tree. In the Art of Ninzuwu teachings a tree is relative to the Dream of the Fahmu, where we are told:

"Know too, that the Fahmu often take the nature of trees,"

The term Fahmu consists of *fa* and *hmu*. Fa is symbolic of a vessel for divine energy, and hmu, the realm of the luminous jewel, Toyotama-hime-no-Mikoto. The sum of Fahmu equals 49, which equals 4 + 9 =13, 1 +3 = 4, or Hmu."

Toyotama-hime-no-Mikoto gave birth to a baby that was later cared for by her younger sister, Tamayori-hime-no-Mikoto. The baby, as discussed earlier, is a symbol of the spiritual fetus. Tamayori-hime-no-Mikoto's care for her elder sister's child is symbolic of how our sacred space is created.

Once the Initiate has entered the Journey of the Crow and reached the Baptism of the Ancient One, as described in the Ivory Tablets of the Crow, a spiritual fetus is conceived. In the ivory Tablets of the Crow, we read:

"It is during the Baptism of the Ancient One that the Goddess revives the spirit. It is like a child being born into this world. When the child is in the womb. It is in this world, but it is in the mother's body. When the child is born it must know how to take care of itself."

When Tamayori-hime-no-Mikoto assumed care for her elder sister's child, it is symbol of the spiritual nourishment we receive from the Divine World through our personal altar, shrine or sacred space. Interestingly, we find this passage in a Wikipedia article, Tamayori-bime:

"Tamayori means Yorishiro, an object to embody Gods. Tamayori-bime is a woman Yorishiro, Miko."

(It should be noted that the terms "hime," and "bime" appearing as a suffix in "divine names" are interchangeable and both have the meaning "princess." The word Hime initially referred to any beautiful female. The antonym of Hime is Shikome (醜女), literally ugly female, though it is archaic and rarely used. Hime is commonly seen as part of a Japanese female divinity's name, such as Toyotama-hime. The Kanji applied to transliterate Hime are 比売 or 毘売 rather than 姫. The masculine counterpart of Hime is Hiko (彦, 比古 or 毘古,) which is seen as part of Japanese male gods' names.)

Based on the information we have discussed so far, Tamayori-hime-no-Mikoto would represent a vehicle of communication with the Divine World. In the Art of Ninzuwu, this would mean creating a shrine in one's home. According to the Dream of the Fahmu, as cited in earlier, this can be found in plants and trees. Creating a personal shrine in the teachings of Ninzuwu-Shinto is building a relationship with a plant or tree, which is used as an intermediary between yourself and the Divine World. This is the teaching in the Dream of the Fahmu.

The Initiate can either find a tree that they can regularly visit in the neighborhood, or they can purchase a small plant for the home. The plant can be to one's own choosing, but should be safe enough to keep in a house with animals. There are many books that have quite a bit of information concerning plants and their metaphysical properties and correspondences. One can also invoke the Shamuzi and inquire of such in this regard.

After the initiate has found or obtained the plant or tree that they would like to use as a personal shrine, they must begin attuning to the energy of the plant or tree. In order to do this, one must know the pattern of how energy flows. Christopher Penczak, in the book entitled, *Spirit Allies*, makes the following observation on page 52 of the said work:

"Esoterically, we usually project *energy* from the *right hand* and receive *energy* from the left, unless we are *left-handed*. Once you understand the *flow* of *energy*, you can control the *flow* of *energy* from each hand and reverse it as needed."

It is generally accepted that right-handed people project energy from the right hand and absorb energy with their left hand. The reverse is true for left-handed people, who project energy with their left hand and absorb energy with their right hand.

The Initiate would use the hand that is yang, which they project energy from, and hold it slightly over the body of the plant or tree while pronouncing the ϩ sign, "eehzz." In the Ivory Tablets of the Crow, we read:

"Know too, that the Fahmu often take the nature of trees and can by spoken to through the mind, and when the ϩ is vibrating upon thy lips."

When we are performing ritual, the plant should be present in the space. It should be positioned, preferably, on the side of the body nearest our projective hand, roughly about twelve to twenty-four inches away. In preparation of ritual, we should attune ourselves to our "botanical shrine," shortly before beginning a sacred work.

The Initiate will see signs of a developing relationship with their living shrine and how such communication affects their lives over time. Interestingly, we find that the world of modern science has found evidence of how closely we can link to plants. In the book, *The Secret Life of Plants*, written by Peter Tompkins and Christopher Bird, we find several essays illustrating "little-known" facts about the capabilities of plants. One researcher, who opened the door for further investigation into this field, is the late Cleve Backster, who was one of America's foremost lie-detector examiners for the United States Government. The book reveals some of Backster's thoughts about the sensitivity of plants, page 10 states:

"Once attuned to a particular person, plants appear to be able to maintain a link with that person, no matter where he went, even among thousands of people. On New Year's Eve in New York City, Backster went out into the bedlam of Times Square armed with a notebook and stopwatch. Mingling with the crowd, he noted his various actions, such as walking, running, going underground by way of subway stairs, nearly getting run over, and having a mild fracas with a news vendor. Back at the lab, he found that each of his three plants, monitored independently, showed similar reactions to his slight emotional adventures."

Ann Evans is a Shinto Priestess, trained at Tsubaki O Kami Yashiro, one of the oldest shrines in Japan. In her book, *Shinto Norito*, she writes:

"The original Shinto shrines in ancient days were sacred groves of trees. Sacred prayers were chanted by the kannushi, or priest, entreating the kami to descend to the sacred location. The tall vertical trees, were the spines upon which the kami would alight."

The Art of Ninzuwu presents the Initiate with a wonderful opportunity to connect with nature and honor of the ancient Shinto tradition.

The Rite of the Dragon Palace

Gazing the Yi Jing is an exercise that strengthens our relationship with the kami and Amaterasu Ohkami. The reader should note that in the Yi Jing Apocrypha of Genghis Khan certain formula are given for the newly-initiated student to practice. In the Art of Ninzuwu, the practice for Gazing the Yi Jing is as follows:

Step 1: Perform steps 1 through 10 in The Armor of Amaterasu Ohkami ritual. Then, for Step 10, invoke the Aum Mudra through all nine chakras and back up to the crown. The Divine World should open up in the mind. Relax.

Step 2: Let yourself sink into the energy wave after invoking the Aum Mudra. Visualize yourself walking in an open field on a bright sunny temple. A radiant gold temple lies ahead of you. Drawing closer you see a woman seated on a throne. It is Amaterasu Ohkami. When you entreat her, she will give you the number of the hexagram.

The Palace of Amaterasu Ohkami is described in the Ivory Tablets of the Crow. Now that we know that Amaterasu Ohkami is the Bride of Nyarzir, we can be aided in the Yi Jing visualization by reading her description in the Ivory Tablets of the Crow:

"Now the Nyarzir is a world with Three Suns and a Green Sky. Every structure is made out of a precious jewel and the roads of the cities are as fine metals. And these cities all stand around the Shining Trapezohedron upon which the Bride of Nyarzir sits upon her Throne.

Nyarzir is a place of instruction for all sorts of miraculous things, and many workers of the mystical arts do often visit and pay tribute to the Bride of Nyarzir for she will teach thee many things in Dreams and the world where the body must breathe."

The World of Nyarzir exists outside of time and space, for its "shadow" is time itself and all that rules this world are merely "shadow elements" of this plane. There are actually two rites, the Purification of Fire and Water and the necessary rite occurs on the "last star" of the month, the Rite of the Dragon Palace.

Step 1: Make a clear space and get into a comfortable position, facing North or East. Use the Cleansing Breathe to clear your mind.

Step 2: Clap three times. Then repeat "Johuta" three times.

Step 3: Perform the Soul of Fire Prayer, as taught in the Ivory Tablets of the Crow, three times.

Step 4: Pray giving thanks to the source of your awareness, Johuta. Give thanks for the use of your awareness. Give thanks to all the "invisible" forces, gods, and guides that have aided you on your spiritual path. Give thanks to the ancestors. Pray for those in need in other areas of the world. Pray for those in need and various situations in your homeland. Pray for the welfare of your family. Pray for friends and co-workers. Pray for one's own being.

Step 5: Clap you hand three times.

Step 6: Two bows, two claps, one bow.

Step 7: Perform the Prayer of Heaven (Amatsu Norito) 3 times:

Prayer of Heaven

Taka ama hari ni Kamu zumari masu Kamurogi Kamuromi no Mikoto moshite
Sumemi oya Kamu Izanagi no Ohkami Tsukushi no Himuka no Tachibana no
Odo no Awagigahara ni Misogi harae tamaishi Toki ne are mase-ru
Harae do no Ohkami tachi Moromoro no Maga goto Tsumi kegare o
Harae tamae Kiyome tamae to Maosu kotono Yoshi o
Amatsu kami Kunitsu kami Yao yorozu no Kami tachi tomo ni Kikoshi mese to
Kashi komi Kashi komi mo mao su

Step 8: Invoke the Aum Mudra then move to Bnhu chakra. Invoke the Bnhu Mudra then move to the Lewhu chakra. Invoke the Lewhu Mudra.

Step 9: The Initiate would then invoke the hexagram that corresponds to the corresponding date of the hexagram by invoking the mudra sentence, next to the said hexagram. For example, the Hexagram of Watatsumi would be invoked. In the Yi Jing Apocrypha of Genghis Khan, it is associated with the Vasuh letter Aum-Shki. This would mean that the Initiate would invoke these to mudras to access that hexagram. Once the hexagram has been access the Initiate can enter this aspect of natural phenomena and commune with its ruler and then proceed on the journey of life.

Step 10: Two bows, two claps, one bow.

The Calendar of Mu is Nyarzir. This calendar consists of eight, forty-five day months, making a total of three-hundred and sixty day calendar. The year begins on the first new moon after the spring equinox. The Initiate in his work must calculate where he is to enter and the signs themselves. There are nine weeks in a month consisting of five days each.

Sign of Amaterasu: Aries- mid-Taurus
Sign of Sheba: Cancer to mid-Leo
Sign of Xuz: Libra to mid-Scorpio
Sign of Watatsumi: Capricorn to mid-Aquarius

Sign of Shamhat: mid-Taurus – Gemini
Sign of Johuta: mid-Leo to Virgo
Sign of Yuvho: mid-Scorpio to Sagittarius
Sign of Nudzuchi: mid-Aquarius – Pisces

The Sign of Amaterasu Ohkami
(Beginning New Moon March 30th 2014)

ZHEE-HAHUN 1	ZHEE-SHAPASH 2	ZHEE-AMATERASU 3	ZHEE-NURU 4	ZHEE-YU NIN 5
AUM-KAGUTSUCHI 6	AUM-FUJIYAMA 7	AUM TENGU 8	☆ 9	AUM-HAHUN 10
TUU SHAPASH 11	TUU AMATERASU 12	TUU-NURU 13	TUU-YU NIN 14	TUU-KATATSUCHI 15
HMU FUJIYAMA 16	HMU TENGU 17	☆ 18	HMU-HAHUN 19	HMU-SHAPASH 20
BNHU AMATERASU 21	BNHU-NURU 22	BNHU YU NIN 23	BNHU KAGUTSUCHI 24	BNHU FUJIYAMA 25
PHE TENGU 26	☆ 27	PHE-HAHUN 28	PHE-SHAPASH 29	PHE-AMATERASU 30
NZU-NURU 31	NZU-YU NIN 32	NZU-KAGUTSUCHI 33	NZU-FUJIYAMA 34	NZU-TENGU 35
☆ 36	LEWHU-HAHUN 37	LEWHU-SHAPASH 38	LEWHU-AMATERASU 39	LEWHU-NURU 40
SHKI-YU NIN 41	SHKI KAGUTSUCHI 42	SHKI-FUJIYAMA 43	SHKI-TENGU 44	☆ 45

The Sign of Shamhat

ZHEE-AOZU 46	ZHEE-ASAKHIRA 47	ZHEE-ZWA 48	ZHEE-CHUKI 49	ZHEE-LALUI 50
AUM-NHU 51	AUM-BURZ 52	AUM-SHAMHAT 53	☆ 54	AUM-AOZU 55
TUU-ASAKHIRA 56	TUU-ZWA 57	TUU-CHUKI 58	TUU-LALUI 59	TUU-NHU 60
HMU-BURZ 61	HMU-SHAMHAT 62	☆ 63	HMU-AOZU 64	HMU-ASAKHIRA 65
BNHU-ZWA 66	BNHU-CHUKI 67	BNHU-LALUI 68	BNHU-NHU 69	BNHU-BURZ 70
PHE-SHAMHAT 71	☆ 72	PHE-AOZU 73	PHE-ASAKHIRA 74	PHE-ZWA 75
NZU-CHUKI 76	NZU-LALUI 77	NZU-NHU 78	NZU-BURZ 79	NZU-SHAMHAT 80
☆ 81	LEWHU-AOZU 82	LEWHU-ASAKHIRA 83	LEWHU-ZWA 84	LEWHU-CHUKI 85
SHKI-LALUI 86	SHKI-NHU 87	SHKI-BURZ 88	SHKI-SHAMHAT 89	☆ 90

The Sign of Sheba

ZHEE-TASUTA 91	ZHEE-KUKUNOCHI 92	ZHEE-IEH 93	ZHEE-GZK 94	ZHEE-JHN 95
AUM-SHEBA 96	AUM-LZWA 97	AUM-KUHVI 98	☆ 99	AUM-TASUTA 100
TUU-KUKUNOCHI 101	TUU-IEH 102	TUU-GZK 103	TUU-JHN 104	TUU-SHEBA 105
HMU-LZWA 106	HMU-KUHVI 107	☆ 108	HMU-TASUTA 109	HMU-KUKUNOCHI 110
BNHU-IEH 111	BNHU-GZK 112	BNHU-JHN 113	BNHU-SHEBA 114	BNHU-LZWA 115
PHE-KUHVI 116	☆ 117	PHE-TASUTA 118	PHE-KUKUNOCHI 119	PHE-IEH 120
NZU-GZK 121	NZU-JHN 122	NZU-SHEBA 123	NZU-LZWA 124	NZU-KUHVI 125
☆ 126	LEWHU-TASUTA 127	LEWHU-KUKUNOCHI 128	LEWHU-IEH 129	LEWHU-GZK 130
SHKI-JHN 131	SHKI-SHEBA 132	SHKI-LZWA 133	SHKI-KUHVI 134	☆ 135

The Sign of Johuta

ZHEE-KOTOAMATSU 136	ZHEE-SUZHA 137	ZHEE-KAMUY-ZI 138	ZHEE-KAYRA-JIN 139	ZHEE-ICHIKISHIMA 140
AUM-ISHITIJIN 141	AUM-NAZIQJIN 142	AUM-INARI 143	☆ 144	AUM-KOTOAMATSU 145
TUU-SUZHA 146	TUU-KAMUY-ZI 147	TUU-KAYRA-JIN 148	TUU-ICHIKISHIMA 149	TUU-ISHITIJIN 150
HMU-NAZIQJIN 151	HMU-INARI 152	☆ 153	HMU-KOTOAMATSU 154	HMU-SUZHA 155
BNHU-KAMUY-ZI 156	BNHU-KAYRA-JIN 157	BNHU-ICHIKISHIMA 158	BNHU-ISHITIJIN 159	BNHU-NAZIQJIN 160
PHE-INARI 161	☆ 162	PHE-KOTOAMATSU 163	PHE-SUZHA 164	PHE-KAMUY-ZI 165
NZU-KAYRA-JIN 166	NZU-ICHIKISHIMA 167	NZU-ISHITIJIN 168	NZU-NAZIQJIN 169	NZU-INARI 170
☆ 171	LEWHU-KOTOAMAU 172	LEWHU-SUZHA 173	LEWHU-KAMUY-ZI 174	LEWHU-KAYRA-JIN 175
SHKI-ICHIKISHIMA 176	SHKI-ISHITIJIN 177	SHKI-NAZIQJIN 178	SHKI-INARI 179	☆ 180

Sign of Xuz

ZHEE-OHOYAMATSUMI 181	ZHEE-NAKAYAMATSUMI 182	ZHEE-HAYAMATSUMI 183	ZHEE-SHIKIYAMATSUMI 184	ZHEE-MASAKATSU-YAMATSUMI 185
AUM-IHASAKU 186	AUM-TAKAWO 187	AUM-XUZ 188	☆ 189	AUM-OHOYAMATSUMI 190
TUU-NAKAYAMATSUMI 191	TUU-HAYAMATSUMI 192	TUU-SHIKIYAMATSUMI 193	TUU-MASAKATSU-YAMATSUMI 194	TUU-IHASAKU 195
HMU-TAKAWO 196	HMU-XUZ 197	☆ 198	HMU-OHOYAMATSUMI 199	HMU-NAKAYAMATSUMI 200
BNHU-HAYAMATSUMI 201	BNHU-SHIKIYAMATSUMI 202	BNHU-MASAKATSU-YAMATSUMI 203	BNHU-IHASAKU 204	BNHU-TAKAWO 205
PHE-XUZ 206	☆ 207	PHE-OHOYAMATSUMI 208	PHE-NAKAYAMATSUMI 209	PHE HAYAMATSUMI 210
NZU-SHIKIYAMATSUMI 211	NZU-MASAKATSU-YAMATSUMI 212	NZU-IHASAKU 213	NZU-TAKAWO 214	NZU-XUZ 215
☆ 216	LEWHU-OHOYAMATSUMI 217	LEWHU-NAKAYAMATSUI 218	LEWHU-HAYAMATSUMI 219	LEWHU-SHIKIYAMATSUMI 220
SHKI-MASAKATSU-YAMATSUMI 221	SHKI-IHASAKU 222	SHKI-TAKAWO 223	SHKI-XUZ 224	☆ 225

Sign of Yuvho

ZHEE-IUT 226	ZHEE-AEUQ 227	ZHEE-JIMMU 228	ZHEE-WOSADO 229	ZHEE-YUVHO 230
AUM-VIYAH 231	AUM-MALUKEDEK 232	AUM-RAIJIN 233	☆ 234	AUM-IUT 235
TUU-AEUQ 236	TUU-JIMMU 237	TUU-WOSADO 238	TUU-YUVHO 239	TUU-VIYAH 240
HMU-MALUKEDEK 241	HMU-RAIJIN 242	☆ 243	HMU-IUT 244	HMU-AEUQ 245
BNHU-JIMMU 246	BNHU-WOSADO 247	BNHU-YUVHO 248	BNHU-VIYAH 249	BNHU-MALUKEDEK 250
PHE-RAIJIN 251	☆ 252	PHE-IUT 253	PHE-AEUQ 254	PHE-JIMMU 255
NZU-WOSADO 256	NZU-YUVHO 257	NZU-VIYAH 258	NZU-MALUKEDEK 259	NZU-RAIJIN 260
☆ 261	LEWHU-IUT 262	LEWHU-AEUQ 263	LEWHU-JIMMU 264	LEWHU-WOSADO 265
SHKI-YUVHO 266	SHKI-VIYAH 267	SHKI-MALUKEDEK 268	SHKI RAIJIN 269	☆ 270

Sign of Watatsumi

ZHEE-MIDZUHANOME 271	ZHEE-SUSANOO 272	ZHEE-NUDZUWATA 273	ZHEE-WATASUMI 274	ZHEE-UGAJIN 275
AUM-AMA-NO-UZUME 276	AUM-IZANAMI 277	AUM-AJISUKITAKAHIKONE 278	☆ 279	AUM-MIDZUHANOME 280
TUU-SUSANOO 281	TUU-NUDZUWATA 282	TUU-WATASUMI 283	TUU-UGAJIN 284	TUU-AMA-NO-UZUME 285
HMU-IZANAMI 286	HMU-AJISUKITAKAHIKONE 287	☆ 288	HMU-MIDZUHANOME 289	HMU-SUSANOO 290
BNHU-NUDZUWATA 291	BNHU-WATASUMI 292	BNHU-UGAJIN 293	BNHU-AMA-NO-UZUME 294	BNHU-IZANAMI 295
PHE-AJISUKITAKAHIKONE 296	☆ 297	PHE-MIDZUHANOME 298	PHE-SUSANOO 299	PHE-NUDZUWATA 300
NZU-WATASUMI 301	NZU-UGAJIN 302	NZU-AMA-NO-UZUME 303	NZU-IZANAMI 304	NZU-AJISUKITAKAHIKONE 305
☆ 306	LEWHU-MIDZUHANOME 307	LEWHU-SUSANOO 308	LEWHU-NUDZUWATA 309	LEWHU-WATASUMI 310
SHKI-UGAJIN 311	SHKI-AMA-NO-UZUME 312	SHKI-IZANAMI 313	SHKI-AJISUKITAKAHIKONE 314	☆ 315

The Sign of Nudzuchi

ZHEE-OROGOROJIMA 316	ZHEE-AHAJI 317	ZHEE-IYONOFUTANA 318	ZHEE-OKI 319	ZHEE-TSUKUSHI 320
AUM-SADO 321	AUM-TSUSHIMA 322	AUM-SHINATOHE 323	☆ 324	AUM-OROGOROJIMA 325
TUU-AHAJI 326	TUU-IYONOFUTANA 327	TUU-OKI 328	TUU-TSUKUSHI 329	TUU-SADO 330
HMU-TSUSHIMA 331	HMU-SHINATOHE 332	☆ 333	HMU-OROGOROJIMA 334	HMU-AHAJI 335
BNHU-IYONOFUTANA 336	BNHU-OKI 337	BNHU-TSUKUSHI 338	BNHU-SADO 339	BNHU-TSUSHIMA 340
PHE-SHINATOHE 341	☆ 342	PHE-OROGOROJIMA 343	PHE-AHAJI 344	PHE-IYONOFUTANA 345
NZU-OKI 346	NZU-TSUKUSHI 347	NZU-SADO 348	NZU-TSUSHIMA 349	NZU-SHINATOHE 350
☆ 351	LEWHU-OROGOROJIMA 352	LEWHU-AHAJI 353	LEWHU-IYONOFUTANA 354	LEWHU-OKI 355
SHKI-TSUKUSHI 356	SHKI-SADO 357	SHKI-TSUSHIMA 358	SHIKI-SHINATOHE 359	☆ 360

The 360-day year would end on March, 25th, 2015, marking a New Year.

The Divine Powers of Nyarzir

The subject of the Calendar of Mu is a very fascinating subject indeed. Unknowing to those outside our tradition, the calendar reflects the interaction of eight known constellation families. These are the Ursa Major, the Zodiac, Perseus, Hercules, Orion, Heavenly Waters, Bayer, and La Caille. For the Initiate, it is a way of walking in the Land of Light while on Earth, bringing Heaven to Earth.

There are a lot of amazing features about this "calendar" and how it can be used. Use if the calendar helps the Initiate grasp some of the concepts held within the Art of Ninzuwu. It is a path of dedication, as one has to invoke the mudras associated with the Vasuh letters, which correspond to the said hexagram, as it appears in the Yi Jing Apocrypha of Genghis Khan. A hexagram is made up of six lines like Amaterasu Ohkami, who is said to shine in the six quarters, North, South, East, West, Above and Below. Therefore, a hexagram is a symbol of a "starry influence," whether it is an ethereal star or a visible one.

The Vasuh letters associated with each hexagram help us to understand the nature of the energy of the star itself. In the Yi Jing Apocrypha of Genghis Khan we learn how the Yi Jing is indeed the Tablets of Destinies. These "Tablets of Destinies" represent the power of the stars. This is revealed in the Enuma Elish, where Tiamat is said to have bestowed "the power of Anu (heaven)" upon Kingu.

The formula for employing the energies of the hexagram is given in the previous section. The Initiate should keep a journal of his/her journey. Intercourse with these energies is not in the same time-space continuum. This means that the Initiate can share in the same experiences by invoking the same hexagram.

Readers may have noticed the ☆ sign on different calendar days, but arranged in some sort of mysterious sequence. This star, called the "Sign of Nyarzir," is symbolic of one spirit, four souls, philosophy discussed earlier in this writing. It also indicates a time when the Initiate can enter into the "Land of Nyarzir." It is not necessary that the Initiate enters into the "Land of Nyarzir" right after the baptism of the Ancient One. They may want to take their time getting familiar with the mudras and etc. The Land of Nyarzir is a rite of perfection. It is a three-hundred and sixty day period that you use to perfect your work. It is also a time for purification.

There are several formulas for purification in the Art of Ninzuwu. The first rite of purification that can be performed on the days of the "Star of Mu," is Johuta the Mirror. These formulas can be practice by the Initiate even if they haven't entered Nyarzir. Below is the formula for the Johuta the Mirror Purification.

Johuta the Mirror

Step 1: Prepare the space for invocation and get into a comfortable position after you have taken all precautionary measures.

Step 2: Three claps.

Step 3: Perform the Opening of the Sea Ceremony. Invoke the Soul of Fire Prayer three times. Call the Shamuzi.

Step 4: Recite the Sword of Ninzuwu incantation and call Wutzki.

Step 5: Recite Johuta the Mirror, as it appears in the Ivory Tablets of the Crow

Step 6: Invoke the Soul of Fire three times. Pray.

Step 7: Three claps.

Readers of the Yi Jing Apocrypha of Genghis Khan may have noticed that use of Reiki symbols in the Book of Nyarzir. Reiki is a unique art that has its origins among the Tengu, and was later revealed to Dr. Usui. Reiki is an art that was originally a purification process. Individuals who are initiated into Reiki and work with the Art of Ninzuwu can re-attune themselves on the days of the "Star of Mu."

There are five "Stars of Mu" in every month. Each Star of Mu is a symbol a certain rite of clairvoyance, which can be exercised at any time. Johuta the Mirror is one out of five purification rites. Takamagahara is the second rite of the "Star of Mu."

Takamagahara Prayer

Step 1: Two bows, two claps, one bow.

Step 2: Recite the Amatsu Norito three times.

Step 3: Invoke the Zhee Mudra through the Nine Chambers and ascend back to Zhee from Shki.

Step 4: Invoke the Celestial Gate (Iyasaka Prayer)

Step 5: Pray

Step 6: Two bows, two claps, one bow.

Iyasaka Prayer

Kuni-no-tokotachi-no-Mikoto, Iyasaka Iyasaka, Iyasaka

Kuni-no-satsuchi-no-Mikoto, Iyasaka Iyasaka, Iyasaka

Toyo-kumo-nu-no-Mikoto, Iyasaka Iyasaka, Iyasaka

Uhijini-no-Mikoto, Suhijini-no-Mikoto, Iyasaka Iyasaka, Iyasaka

Otonoji-no-Mikoto, Otomabe-no-Mikoto, Iyasaka Iyasaka, Iyasaka

Omo-Daru-no-Mikoto, Kashiko-ne-no-Mikoto, Iyasaka Iyasaka, Iyasaka

The third "Star of Mu" is the Key of Omohi-kane-no-Kami. He is a power without a sign, but very useful in aiding the Initiate in divining matters that may cause stress. Promotes clear thinking and reveals the forces behind logical patterns. Useful in warding off negative thoughts. The Encyclopedia of Shinto states the following in regard to Omohi-kane-no-Kami:

"An offspring of the kami Takamimusuhi, and endowed with the ability to "think together" (omoi-kane) about various things. In Sendai kuji hongi, the kami's name is also given as Yagokoro Omoikane no kami ("the kami that thinks together myriad thoughts"). At the time Amaterasu hid away in the Rock Cave of Heaven, Omoikane considered various measures to draw her out again, leading to the successful return of Amaterasu to the world."

The Key of Omohi-kane-no-Kami

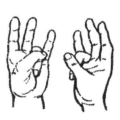

Step 1: Two bows, two claps, one bow.

Step 2: Recite the Amatsu Norito three times

Step 3: Hold the Key of Omohi-kane-no-Kami while chanting "Omohi-kane-no-Kami," three times in each chamber, starting with the Zhee chakra descending down to Shki.

Step 4: Perform the Cleansing Breath while still holding the Key of Omohi-kane-no-Kami.

Step 5: Begin chant "Omohi-kane-no-Kami," three times for each chamber, ascending from the Shki chakra to Zhee.

Step 6: Two bows, two claps, one bow.

The fourth "Star of Mu" is the "Fire of Ninzuwu Chant." This chant is very simple, but effective in riding oneself of toxic thoughts and physical habits.

Fire of Ninzuwu Chant

Step 1: Clap your hands three times.

Step 2: Recite the word "Johuta" three times.

Step 4: Perform the Soul of Fire once for every chamber, starting with Zhee and descending down to Shki.

Step 5: Perform the Cleansing Breath.

Step 6: Perform the Soul of Fire once for every chamber, starting from Shki ascending back up to Zhee.

Step 7: Three claps.

The fifth and final "Star of Mu' is the Chant of Heavenly Numbers. The chant consists of numbers that are linked to a deep esoteric meaning. William E. Griffis, in the book, *The Mikado's Empire,* analyzes the mythology of Amaterasu Ohkami's retreat in the rock-cave, and what it took to get her out. One kami, Ame-no-Uzume-no-Mikoto, had begun to dance in an enchanting fashion. Griffis states in his work:

"As she danced, the drum-like spirit prepared for her resounded, and she, becoming possessed by a spirit of folly, sung a song in verses of six syllables each..."

This song is described also in the footnotes of W. G. Aston's version of the Nihon Shoki:

"In Hirata's version of the ancient mythical narrative, he introduces here an incantation said in the "Kojiki" to have been taught by the Sun-Goddess to Ninigi no Mikoto, but stated in the "Ko-go-jiui" to have come down originally from Uzume no Mikoto. It consists of the syllables Hito-futa-mi-yo-itsu-mu-nana-ya-kokono-tari, which Hirata has tried hard to extract some meaning of it."

Aston continues to explain that the meaning of these syllables is known ad relates to numbers. The chant is as follows: Hito, Futa, Mi, Yo, Itsu, Muyu, Nana, Ya, Kokono, Tari, Momo, Chi, Yorozu. The meaning of this chant is analyzed deeply in the teachings of Ōnisaburō Deguchi:

"Literally meaning "the Chant of Heavenly Numbers," Ama-no-Kazu-Uta is a prayer that invokes the mystical power of kototama (or kotodama), thereby providing those who intone the incantation with divine help and the grace of Kami.

In this respect, Ama-no-Kazu-Uta is by no means a mere sequence of numbers; instead, it praises the

Great Original Spirit (= the primordial form of the Great Original Deity of the Universe) represented by kototama "su" for Its Virtue, Power and Glory in creating and evolving the cosmos through a myriad of times, stages and processes.
(Note: the Great Original Spirit is identical to Ame-no-Minaka-Nushi-no-Kami (The Deity Master-of-the August-Center-of-Heaven) in the Kojiki (Records of Ancient Matters) and to Ame-no-Minehio-no-Kami (The Deity Fire-of-the August-Peak-of-Heaven) in the Reikai Monogatari.)

Hito (1) = ichi-rei-shi-kon (four aspects of man's soul governed by one direct portion of the Spirit of Kami)
The Great Original Spirit, the root cause of the great cosmos, governs the four soul-aspects, and, under the command of the direct portion of the Spirit called.

Futa (2) = hachi-riki (eight forces of the True God)
Varying degrees of the union of yin and yang, which constitutes a part of the workings of the True Kami, result in eight forces--namely, do (activating force), sei (quieting force), kai (melting force), gyo (coagulating force), in (pulling force), chi (loosening force), go (combining force) and bun (dividing force).

Mi (3) = san-gen (three irreducible elements of the physical world)
Subtle and intricate combinations of the eight forces produce the three fundamental elements of the material plane, go (tamatsume-musubi = generative power of Kami that fastens the soul in the physical body; essence of minerals), ju (taru-musubi = generative power of Kami that enriches creatures; essense of plants) and ryu (iku-musubi = generative power of Kami that gives life to inanimate objects; essence of animals).

Incidentally, Onisaburo indicates that the chemical elements which have been discovered until today will ultimately fall into these three categories. He goes on to say that go corresponds to Kuni-no-Toko-Tachi-no-Kami (The Earthly-Eternally-Standing-Deity) in Kojiki, ju, to Toyo-Kumonu-no-Kami (The Luxuriant-Integrating-Master-Deity) and ryu, to Umashi-Ashikabi-Hikoji-no-Kami (The Pleasant-Reed-Shoot-Prince-Elder-Deity).

Hito also means the Spirit of the True God (ichi-rei-shi-kon), futa, His Power (hachi-riki) and mi, His Body (san-gen). Thus, at this stage, the three irreducible elements of the universe, or the Three Attributes of the Godhead, are all present.

Yo (4) = yo (world) (this is a homonym; the same applies to the rest of the numbers) A mud-like world comes into being.

Itsu (5) = itsu (emergence) The sun, the moon, the stars and the earth appear.

Muyu (6) = muyu (multiplication) Plants, trees, animals and various other creatures proliferate.

Nana (7) = nana (fulfillment of the earth) The birth of human beings realizes the kingdom of the earth.

Ya (8) = ya (prosperity) The world flourishes continually and expansively.

Kokono (9) = kokono (solidification) The fullness and stability of the world are strengthened.

Tari (10) = tari (completion) The world reaches perfection. (The True Kami desires that the world evolve in the manner of upward spiral, treading the path from perfection to greater perfection.)

Momo (100) = momo (variety) Various other things are further created.

Chi (1000) = chi (blood = spirit) The blood (or spirit) of the great creation work circulates in every vein of the universe, constantly replenishing all entities with vigor and vitality.

Yorozu (10000) = yorozu (departure from darkness) The world of illuminous light unfolds forever and ever via the evolutionary process explained thus far."

The Chant of Heavenly Numbers

Step 1: Two Bows, two claps, one bow.

Step 2: Perform the Amatsu Norito three times.

Step 3: Recite Hito, Futa, Mi, Yo, Itsu, Muyu, Nana, Ya, Kokono, Tari, Momo, Chi, Yorozu – three times at each chamber, starting at Zhee and descending down to Shki.

Step 4: Perform the Cleansing Breath.

Step 5: Recite Hito, Futa, Mi, Yo, Itsu, Muyu, Nana, Ya, Kokono, Tari, Momo, Chi, Yorozu – three times at each chamber, starting at Shki and ascending up to Zhee.

Step 6: Pray

Step 7: Two bows, two claps, one bow.

The Art of the Crow (Teleportation)

When the Initiate sets his/her heart on the great work, they are provided with the necessary tools to aid in such from the Divine World. None of the methods appearing in this text can be accessed by those "who are just looking to see what happens." This is especially true when it comes to the Art of Teleportation.

Like our mother Amaterasu Ohkami, the Initiate can let their consciousness shine into matters that supersede the laws of time and space. One must have a purpose in the use of this art, or it will cause a "kick back" in the person's day-to-day experience. Usually, we encounter the "rough side of the kami" first, also known as ara-mitama. This means that as we progress in our development, the appearance of the kami will change also. We attract what we invite, but we speak more loudly to "invisible forces" by means of our emotional state.

The Art of the Crow is a special incantation that helps us in our cultivation of a state of being called immortality. While it may seem like a simple chant it is filled with deep meaning, as the forces invoke relate to the pole star. It is a work of the marvelous and can be performed when necessary

The Art of the Crow (long version)

Step 1: Two bows, two claps, one bow

Step 2: Perform the Opening of the Sea

Step 3: Perform the Soul of Fire Prayer

Step 4: Perform the Calling of the Shamuzi:

Step 5: Recite the Sword of Ninzuwu Incantation

Step 6: Recite the Amatsu Norito three times

Step 7: Invoke the Armor of Amaterasu Ohkami (the Nine Mudras)

Step 8: Recite the names Ame-no-Minaka-Nushi-no-kami, Takami-musubi-no-kami, Kami-musubi-no-kami, in a row, and once for every chakra, beginning with Zhee and descending down to Shki.

Step 9: Give thanks in prayer. You will feel a wave of energy. Let your consciousness float in the sea of energy, as your body upon water. Focus on the matter at hand, but keep the mind relaxed and the vision will open up and the Initiate will be able to see clearly an experience that is not within his/her physical grasp. It is here that one can exercise their intentions in accordance with the divine world.

Step 11: Perform the Cleansing Breath

Step 12: Two bows, two claps, one bow.

Editor's Notes

This text is for the advanced practitioner of the Art of Ninzuwu. If you have received this text and have not studied the practices in the Ivory Tablets of the Crow or the Yi Jing Apocrypha of Genghis Khan, I would suggest that you invest some time and study into these practices first. Wisdom cannot be rushed. This is not a text where someone learns how to do the techniques listed in this book and=use such for their aims. You must be initiated in the prior step before implementing this into your work. If you are a student in the Art of Ninzuwu teachings, it is strongly advise that you consult you mentor before attempting to make use of this text.

There were many discussions about how to release this material, and should it be released in public. One thing that was heavily considered, and a large reason why the text was publicly released, had a lot to do with supporters of the Ivory Tablets of the Crow. Many, who bought the Ivory Tablets never studied with our group. Maybe they could grasp the symbolism and have chosen to work in solitude. They could perhaps be sincere individuals who have contacted their inner "soul of fire" and understand the workings of the Art of Ninzuwu Tradition.

These teachings are not for selfish purposes, but for the advancement and evolution of all humanity. These are some of the things taught in the deeper chambers of the Shrine of Ninzuwu's agenda.

After working with the system for quite some time, I must say that it is an effective means of transformation, the strongest that I have ever experienced. The Art of Ninzuwu consists of three levels, which are all interchangeable. First, there is the initiatory path outlined in the Ivory Tablets of the Crow. This gives one a basic understanding of some of the practices and understanding of Ninzuwu on an initiatory level.

Next, we have the Yi Jing Apocrypha of Genghis Khan. This text reveals some things about the Initiate's path, in terms of Ninzuwu, and provides some basic information as to how these practices are connected to Shinto.

The Armor of Amaterasu Ohkami is the epitome of the Art of Ninzuwu's public teachings, and relates heavily to the information found in the Ivory Tablets of the Crow. It explores the depth and heart of mystical Shinto practice.

Here are a few notes on pronunciation of some of the names and words in Japanese. It is based on the pronunciation guide found in Shinto Norito by Ann Llewellyn Evans, a marvelous book indeed.

>a pronounced like [a} in "father"
>i pronounced like [ee] in "meet"
>u pronounced like [oo] in "boot"
>e pronounced like [e] in "met"
>o pronounced like [o] in "over"

ABOUT THE AUTHOR

Messiah-el Bey is a resident of New York City. He has been teaching the Art of Ninzuwu for over two years and has been a student of ancient Mesopotamian and Japanese spirituality for over 15 years.

Made in the USA
Lexington, KY
28 March 2015